W9-DAA-645

THE BOOK OF
Lost Recipes

*The Best Signature Dishes
From Historic Restaurants Rediscovered*

JAYA SAXENA

co-founder of Uncommon Courtesy

PAGE STREET
PUBLISHING CO.

PAGE STREET
PUBLISHING CO.

First published in 2016 by
Page Street Publishing Co.
27 Congress Street, Suite 103
Salem, MA 01970
www.pagestreetpublishing.com

Distributed by Macmillan, sales in Canada by The Canadian Manda Group.

19   18   17   16   1   2   3   4   5

ISBN13: 978-1-62414-239-0
ISBN10: 1-62414-239-7

Library of Congress Control Number: 2015952106

Cover and book design by Page Street Publishing Co.
Food photography by Jennifer Blume
Historical images: see page 235

Printed and bound in China

Page Street is proud to be a member of 1% for the Planet. Members donate one percent
of their sales to one or more of the over 1,500 environmental and sustainability charities
across the globe who participate in this program.

To my parents, for all of your support, and to Matt,
for your enduring love and willingness to eat
a bunch of weird, historic dishes

INTRODUCTION

———•———

Think of the restaurant that changed your life. Is that too dramatic? Maybe it's the diner you went to every night in high school, or the place you saved up every penny to eat at, or just the place you always return to when it's been too long. It may have been famous, historic or new, or it may just have been there, but whatever it was, it was yours. Mine is an old Italian place in New York's East Village, Lanza's. It's where there are trompe l'oeil paintings of Mt. Vesuvius on the walls and it's not uncommon to hear the *Godfather* theme playing softly in the backyard. I order a carafe of house wine and the special spaghetti with tomatoes and thick chunks of mozzarella, or the mozzarella in carrozza with what I maintain is the best marinara sauce in the city. Many places probably make all these things just as well, but that will never matter to me.

Restaurants are inherently special. The experience of dining out is still a relatively new one, and even in instances where it's a necessity (for quick lunches during work, for any food at all if one's apartment lacks a kitchen), it still feels like a treat. It's about the food, but it's about more than that—atmosphere, community, class. Thus, what we seek in a restaurant, "our" restaurants, is somewhat aspirational, and when they succeed it's because they've tapped into the needs and desires of a place and time. *The Book of Lost Recipes* is about places that did just that.

When researching the restaurants in this book, I was driven by the question "What made this place *this place*?" What made it famous, or beloved, or kept it in the hearts and minds of its community long after the doors shut? The goal here is to provide a glimpse into the differences, and similarities, of dining culture around America in the 20th century, because dining culture is unique from food culture as a whole. What people make in the home is not what they crave in a restaurant.

Exactly what we are looking for and respond to in a restaurant changes by region, year, economy and a number of other factors, but there is one thing that they all seem to have in common: comfort. Comfort comes in many forms. In some places, it's a restaurant opened by immigrants, serving the food of a home country to people who couldn't find it elsewhere. In others, it's fine-dining establishments that know how to gently introduce new flavors to a posh audience. Sometimes it's a charming owner or a trusted family who become pillars of their communities. Sometimes it's about providing for the ignored or oppressed. And sometimes it's just about being reliable, being good and being there. In all cases, these restaurants reflect our populations, our economy, our views on race and class, and our aspirations. These swirl together and, for moments sometimes too brief, make these places something more.

Lanza's also happens to be one of the last relics of a dying population. The East Village has changed in the hundred-plus years since Lanza's opened. The Italians largely moved out, and new people moved in, bringing with them the types of businesses they want to frequent, whether you call that gentrification or the hand of the free market. Lanza's stands with a few other institutions, the sole survivors of a slew of others that looked just like them. It represents a success, for now, in a familiar story of failure. Or really, a story of preservation in a familiar story of change.

Things, indeed, have changed. A common refrain I heard in my research is that we have lost dining out as an experience. I don't think that's the case. We have made tremendous gains in this pocket of society, whether it's the growing respect for diverse cultures and cuisines, an increasingly adventurous national palate, or just the fact that our restaurants are no longer segregated. Many things have changed for the better. But certainly there are things we have lost. There are places here that could not be built today. Populations move and change, economies rise and fall, and the conditions that spelled success for a restaurant can just as quickly spell its demise. *The Book of Lost Recipes* is about the places now remembered as special. Sometimes they were famous, sometimes they weren't, and in some cases, they were strange vestiges of times we'd rather forget.

The Book of Lost Recipes is about this change, but it's also about—what else—the food. Whatever other factors came into play, the fact is none of these places would have been as beloved if what they were serving wasn't good. And as much as the book is a glimpse into dining culture, it's also a glimpse into America's changing dining preferences. We see the days when an elaborate Baked Lobster Savannah was the peak of elegance, rather than anything described as "molecular gastronomy." When chili was the hot new food sweeping Oregon. When the people of Detroit would spend their hot summer Sundays boating across the river for fresh frog legs.

We may have lost the restaurants, but luckily, in some cases, the food can be resurrected. With a bite of chopped liver we can picture the Romanian Steakhouse on Manhattan's Lower East Side where Jewish vaudeville stars danced to klezmer. With a sip of punch we can imagine the Tiki behemoth towering over Columbus, Ohio. With a curried meatball we can see the leaps and bounds Indian cuisine has made in fifty years. By cooking and tasting what we ate, we can start to answer the questions of why we ate it, and sometimes ask ourselves why we stopped in the first place.

The recipes in this book are representative of their own places and times, enhanced by the context of their histories. They are also good recipes. Some may be familiar and others may be complete throwbacks, or may even feel entirely new, but they are the things memories are made of. Think back to your restaurant, the dish that captured your attention, the one that you go back to whenever you need it, or wish you could go back to. These dishes were those things for someone of a different time, and making them connects us to the lives and past of a place we would have never otherwise experienced. It is quite possibly the best way to time travel.

Century Inn

Scenery Hill, PA

Opened 1788

———·———

Originally, towns along Braddock Road were twelve miles (19 km) apart. That's because twelve miles was as long as your average oxen could travel in a day. Braddock Road bled into the National Road, and was used as a stagecoach line, the only road funneling anyone from east to west in the area. Stephen and Thomas Hill, the owners of the stagecoach company, knew this gave them a captive audience and in 1788 began building Hill's Tavern.

Officially founded in 1794, Hill's Tavern, now known as the Century Inn, has been continuously operating as similar inns and taverns on the road fell away. "At one point there were four other Inns in the village. We're the only one left because we are a stone building," says Megin Harrington, whose family currently owns the inn. "All the stone was quarried on our property. We went through so many changes, and other buildings' changes did not hold up."

The impressive architecture also attracted a richer clientele, like Andrew Jackson, James K. Polk and General Santa Anna. President Abraham Lincoln even hired a coach to take him there, even though he was staying at a different inn down the road, just because he heard the breakfast was so good. In 1811 parts of Braddock Road were paved over and expanded to make the National Road, the first highway built by the national government. It funneled thousands of settlers westward, many of whom would continue to stop at the tavern for meals along the way. There were also rooms on the property for people to stay overnight, though according to the original rules of the house, there were "no more than five to a bed."

In the tavern, a flag from the Whiskey Rebellion, which took place the same year the Inn was being built, still hangs. At that time, farmers in the area had discovered they could distill their surplus grains and sell the product in Philadelphia for extra money, or just trade it among themselves. At the time, liquor and beer were safer to drink than water, and paired with the common belief that alcohol contained medicinal properties, the market was ripe for whiskey. Concurrently, the federal government found itself in debt from the recent wars and decided taxing whiskey would be a quick and easy way to make some of that money back. This didn't please the local farmers, who rebelled, but were soon quashed by thousands of George Washington's troops. And though the whiskey tax was repealed by the early 1800s, the rebellion was the first demonstration of the power of the new national government.

The Harringtons bought the inn in 1945 and resisted pressure to update the decor. By 1952, a historic marker to the tavern was erected on Route 40 (which encompasses much of the National Road) and today they still serve meals to weary travelers. "We have a lot of lamb, duck and pheasant. We use things that would have been readily available in colonial times," says Harrington. Over 200 years out, the road has changed. It's easier to just keep driving west, to the next big city or the next gas station, sticking to what one knows. Places like the Century Inn remind one of what's still around if one takes a moment to look.

Century Inn Braised Lamb Shank

The Century Inn primarily uses products that would have been available during the early days of the inn, and this lamb shank is a great example of both the ingredients of the area and the type of warm, hearty food the inn has served over the years. The lamb is cooked until it falls off the bone in a simple, velvety sauce that would satisfy any traveler, then or now.

Serves 6

6 lamb hind shanks

1 pinch kosher salt

1 pinch cracked black pepper

¼ cup (32 g) all-purpose flour

¼ cup (60 ml) vegetable oil

1 cup (240 g) onions, diced

½ cup (120 g) celery, diced

½ cup (120 g) carrots, diced

½ cup (118 ml) dry red wine

1 qt (950 ml) veal or beef stock

1 bay leaf

Preheat the oven to 350°F (176°C). Season the lamb shanks with salt and pepper. Dredge with the flour, and pat off the excess. Heat the vegetable oil in a high-sided roasting pan over medium heat. Add the lamb shanks to the pan, being careful not to crowd, and brown them on all sides. Remove the shanks and add the onions, celery, and carrots to the pan. Cook until they begin to caramelize, about 10 minutes, then deglaze with the red wine. Bring the mixture to a simmer until most of the wine has evaporated, about 3 to 4 minutes. Return the lamb shanks to the pan and add the stock and bay leaf. Bring to a boil, and cover with foil or a tight-fitting lid. Place in the oven and cook for 2 to 3 hours, turning the shanks incrementally. Add more stock or water if the juice seems to be evaporating too quickly. When done, the meat should be able to be removed from the bone with a fork.

Remove the shanks and pour sauce into a sauce pot. Reduce until the sauce is thickened, for about 15 minutes, enough to coat the back of a spoon. Serve shanks with sauce on top.

[1] For reference information see Endnotes.

CENTURY INN PEANUT SOUP

The Century Inn's peanut soup is a long-standing tradition, and some claim it's based on a recipe from Thomas Jefferson. Whether or not that's true, peanuts were a popular crop in the American South, so whenever they were shipped north they were a real treat. Peanut soup was a common recipe in American cookbooks in the late 18th century, and this recipe honors that tradition, while modernizing the flavor profile a bit with lime and soy sauce.

SERVES 4

1 tbsp (15 ml) vegetable oil

½ cup (120 g) celery, diced

½ cup (120 g) onions, diced

3 cups (709 ml) chicken stock

Juice of 1 lime

1 tsp (5 ml) soy sauce

1 cup (240 g) ground roasted peanuts (or low sodium peanut butter)

1 cup (236 ml) heavy cream

Salt to taste

Chopped peanuts for garnish

In a medium sauce pan, heat the vegetable oil, and sauté the celery and onions until the onions are translucent, about 10 minutes. Add the chicken stock, lime juice and soy sauce, and bring the mixture to a boil. Whisk in the peanuts a bit at a time until the mixture is thickened, and simmer for another 5 minutes. Remove from the heat. Whisk in the heavy cream until the soup is just thick enough to coat the back of a spoon. Add salt to taste and garnish with chopped peanuts and serve.

[2] For reference information see Endnotes.

PLANTERS HOTEL

New York, NY

1833-1940s

What would you do if you found out your favorite restaurant was haunted? Well, it probably wouldn't happen because you'd likely get kicked out before they locked the doors at night and unleashed the night stalkers. But according to "Phantom at the Planters, 1833–1933, our first hundred years," a strange piece of advertisement,[3] that's exactly what happened at the Planters Hotel in 1933.

The Planters Hotel was located on Greenwich and Albany streets in downtown Manhattan (though one account puts[4] it at Greenwich and Cedar), and it was popular with travelers from the South—such as Daniel Webster, Aaron Burr, John C. Calhoun and eventually Edgar Allen Poe—who were looking for good food and a good night's rest. Its proximity to the Perth Amboy ferry made it particularly appealing. "Here the first cotton exchange in America was established, where thousands of dollars worth of cargoes changed hands every year," wrote one history by H. Jerome Parker.[5] Though New York outlawed slave trafficking in 1792, it was at places like these that the city maintained powerful economic ties with the plantation South. However, the Civil War put an end to that exchange, and the hotel closed until a new owner (possibly D. Clinton Mackey, a surety bondsman named as the owner when he died in 1932)[6] opened it as Planters Cafeteria and Restaurant in 1922.

This is where we find our pamphlet's haunted protagonist, who claims he awoke alone in the restaurant and decided to take a walk around. On the second floor he encountered a man who "looked almost too old to be alive, and had a bearing which we associate with years long before the jazz age." The man offered him a pipe, and said, "I have been here since 1833. Exactly one hundred years ago tonight, I was among the first guests to dine here." In the story, the ghost continues to explain the history of Planters and New York. He reminds us that this was no "little back street" in 1833, and when asked how they lived without "subways, radios, airships" and "how long you had to wait for news," he replies, "We didn't need any news. We had our own lives to live and we lived them leisurely and well."

But what of the food? The menu of the original Planters sounds pretty incredible. The ghost describes "roast haunch of venison…with currant jelly sauce melted in port wine," roast leg of pork brushed in oil and applesauce, baked shad with butter gravy, and "roast pheasant…stuffed with minced snipe and truffles and served with a decoration of oranges." It was certainly heavy food, but also a touch more elaborate than what you'd find at your average chophouse, meant both to sate travelers and impress potential clients.

Through the 1920s and 1930s, Planters continued to be a popular restaurant and the kind of place where business would be done over food, as it had been when it was a hotel. But, as H. Jerome Parker wrote, "you eat heartily as did Webster, Calhoun and Poe—still you experience a feeling of emptiness—something seems missing." Even then the "real days" of the Planters seemed gone, and it was relying on that perennial New York hobby—nostalgia. By 1939, a New York City guide called it[7] a "relic of the old days," and from then it didn't last long. But when you walk in downtown New York, the ghosts of the Planters may still be there.

PLANTERS HOTEL-STYLE ROAST PORK

The ghost at the Planters Hotel described one of their delicacies as a "roast leg of pork brushed in oil, roasted for three hours, served with applesauce." It's a simple dish, but a classic sweet and savory pairing, made even more appealing by the pork's puffed, crisped skin. It's a dish that's stayed appealing through the centuries. Be sure to save any leftovers for day-after sandwiches.

SERVES 8-10

1 leg of pork, about 15–20 lbs (6.8–9 kg)

4–5 tbsp (20–25 ml) of vegetable or sunflower oil

Salt and pepper to taste

½ cup (118 ml) of applesauce

Preheat the oven to 450°F (232°C). Lightly score the skin of the pork leg with a knife in a criss-cross pattern, being sure not to pierce all the way through to the meat, and brush it with a neutral oil like vegetable or sunflower. Season the leg heavily with salt and pepper, and roast it for half an hour until skin is crispy, then lower the temperature to 350°F (176°C). Continue roasting for approximately 3 hours, until the inner temperature reaches 145°F (63°C), and the skin is nicely browned and crisp. Let rest for 1 hour, then serve with the applesauce.

[8] For reference information see Endnotes.

PLANTERS HOTEL-STYLE ROAST VENISON WITH CURRANT PORT SAUCE

The haunch of the venison is the hind leg, also known as the Denver leg, which can be ordered from many specialty stores or butchers. This method results in perfectly pink meat under a salty crust. It's served with a sweet-and-sour sauce that cuts the gaminess, and makes for great sandwiches the next day.

SERVES 8-10

1 haunch of venison, boned and rolled, about 5 lbs (2.2 kg)

¼ cup (45 g) kosher salt

Vegetable oil

½ cup (120 g) currant jelly

½ cup (118 ml) port

Preheat the oven to 425°F (218°C). Let the venison come to room temperature, pat dry and rub all over with kosher salt, enough so that the crystals are still visible. Place the meat in the rack of a large roasting tray and brush all over with oil. Pour a little water in the bottom of the tray to keep the drippings from smoking. Roast for 20 minutes. Turn heat down to 325°F (162°C) and roast for another 45 minutes, basting with more oil occasionally until the roast reaches about 130°F (54°C) measured with a meat thermometer. Remove the roast from the oven and let rest.

Pour meat drippings into a pan with the currant jelly and port wine. Reduce until the sauce coats the back of a spoon, about 7 minutes. Serve over sliced venison.

[8] For reference information see Endnotes.

HARVEY'S FAMOUS RESTAURANT

Washington, DC

1858-1990s

———•———

Everyone seems to have a different theory on how Harvey's Famous Restaurant, the go-to seafood spot for Washington, D.C.'s elite from 1858 through the 1970s, came up with its famed steamed oysters. One theory is that it was an accident facilitated by a leaky steam jet in the basement of the Harvey brothers' first restaurant[9], which they opened when George Washington Harvey was only sixteen. The steam blasted a pile of nearby oysters, and the Harveys discovered they tasted a lot like their popular roasted oysters. Another is that George Washington Harvey had them at a dinner party hosted by Mrs. Frances Seward, wife of Secretary of State William H. Seward, and decided to add them to the menu.[10] Yet another is that patrons were too impatient to wait for Harvey's famous oysters to be roasted, so they just came up with a steaming method.[11] Or perhaps those patrons were hungry Civil War soldiers, craving something other than the hardtack and coffee they had been living on in the fields.[12]

Whatever the story, Harvey's Famous Restaurant earned its name. In its heyday it was the most well-known restaurant in Washington D.C., where the political elite met and networked over shellfish and cocktails (their menu makes the claim they were the originators of the Jack Rose). According to *The History of Harvey's*, "whenever the pressure of public business would permit, [Ulysses S. Grant] would leave the White House and walk down the avenue to Harvey's. ...a peck of 'steamed' was his usual order, over which he lingered with the enjoyment of a connoisseur." The Canvasback Club, a meeting of the likes of Thomas Nast and members of the New York delegation of Congress, also made Harvey's their meeting place, and in 1902 presented George Harvey with a silver flagon as a symbol of their appreciation.

Originally known as Harvey's Ladies' and Gentlemen's Oyster Saloon, it occupied three floors on the corner of Pennsylvania Avenue and 11th Street—the first floor public bar and restaurant for men, the second floor ladies' dining room, and the third floor private dining room, though late nights it would turn into a dance floor with a live jazz band. According to one account, "Harvey was an old-fashioned landlord who liked to wander among his guests at the table and see that they were well cared for," occasionally saucing dishes in front of guests if he believed it hadn't been done properly. Oysters were only to be harvested from the Chesapeake Bay, and he considered the oyster, the diamondback terrapin and the canvasback duck "the Creator's greatest gifts to mankind." George Harvey allegedly estimated that he had sold a billion oysters in the 1906 season.[13]

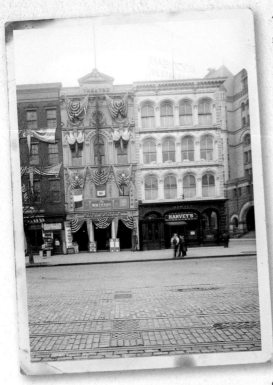

That was the same year George Harvey sold out the business and retired, and in 1909 he died of heart failure. But the business went on, serving the D.C. elite as much diamondback terrapin and seafood as ever. In 1931 Harvey's was pushed out of its historic building, and moved to Connecticut Avenue, next to the Mayflower hotel, where it continued successfully. However, in the 1970s it was forced out again due to Metro construction, and moved to 18th and K streets. It continued there through the 1990s, but without its historic surroundings, it could only rely on its food, which was expensive. Too expensive, it seems, to coincide with the recession of the early 1990s.

When Harvey's opened, oysters were a cheap street food, raked from the bay by the barrel and sold out of carts. Early American cookbooks list recipes for oysters many wouldn't dream of making now, from oyster omelets to oyster hash to oyster mousse, anything to utilize this affordable source of protein. In 1884, 15 million bushels were harvested, supplying almost half the world's demand for oysters, and earning them the nickname "Chesapeake gold." Naturally, a gold rush followed, and the "Oyster Wars"[14] nearly destroyed the bay's oyster beds. Fisherman from New England sailed south, poaching local watermen's territory. Men were killed over this greed, and the oysters suffered. By 1889, the oyster population in the bay had declined by a third, and in 2010, just under 200,000 bushels were harvested. It was due to this over-harvesting that the oyster's place in American food culture drastically changed. Through the 20th century it became too rare to be an everyday snack, and instead turned into the chosen appetizer of the elite. And in a recession, not everyone could afford that luxury anymore.

HARVEY'S JACK ROSE COCKTAIL

Harvey's claims to have invented this cocktail, though there's been some debate on the topic. Some sources say it was a bartender in New Jersey, while others say it was a case of multiple discovery. But Harvey's certainly called it its own, and it was very popular. The fruity combination stays refreshing instead of overly sweet, making it an excellent accompaniment for seafood, or just on its own.

SERVES 1

2 oz (50 ml) applejack

1 oz (25 ml) lime juice

½ oz (12 ml) grenadine

Twist of lime, for garnish

Shake ingredients, except garnish, over ice, and strain into a martini glass. Garnish with a twist of lime.

HARVEY'S IMPERIAL CRAB

This recipe came from a promotional pamphlet called The History of Harvey's, *which listed only the instructions
"Mix crab lump with mayonnaise, add capers, season to taste, bake well in shell." This version stays true to a recipe that
emphasizes thick chunks of crab meat over breading and other fillers, because why eat bread when you can eat crab?
Also, baking this in crab shells is certainly an elegant way to serve it, but it can also be made in small ramekins.
Note: the capers mean this recipe rarely needs extra salt.*

SERVES 2

½ cup (120 g) lump crab meat (fresh is best, though canned will do), drained

¼ cup (60 ml) mayonnaise

1 tbsp (15 g) capers

¼ tsp Old Bay

Black pepper to taste

1 tsp (5 g) breadcrumbs

Preheat the oven to 400°F (204°C). If using crab meat from fresh crabs, break open the shell and scoop out meat, making sure to leave a neat opening in the shell to stuff later. Remove the legs and scrape meat from there as well. Mix the meat well with mayonnaise, capers, Old Bay and pepper. Split the filling evenly between crab shells or ramekins, and pile high. Top with breadcrumbs and bake for 20 minutes, until the top is well browned.

[15] For reference information see Endnotes.

HARVEY'S STEAMED OYSTERS
WITH "HARVEY" SAUCE

Harvey served his oysters with a combination of melted butter and his proprietary "Harvey" oyster sauce, prepared tableside. A cross between spicy ketchup and cocktail sauce, it'll work well on almost everything on the raw bar, especially these delicate steamed oysters—Harvey's specialty.

SERVES 2

12 fresh oysters, preferably from the Chesapeake Bay

2 tbsp (30 g) butter

¼ tsp paprika

1 tbsp (15 ml) Worcestershire sauce

3 tbsp (44 ml) ketchup

Dash of tabasco

Salt and pepper to taste

Arrange the oysters in a steaming basket so they do not overlap. Steam the oysters until all the shells have opened, about 10 minutes. Once open, steam for an additional 5 minutes.

For the sauce, melt the butter, then whisk in the rest of the ingredients, seasoning with salt and pepper to taste. Serve the oysters with Harvey sauce on the side, for dipping.

[16] For reference information see Endnotes.

SCHWEIZER'S

Detroit, MI
1862-1983

———•———

Between 1860 and 1890, Detroit's population grew from around 45,000 to over 200,000, making it the 15th largest city in America.[17] A large part of that was due to German immigration, fueled by the revolutions of 1848, and many flocked to areas with a strong manufacturing sector. Detroit was a natural settling place, and by 1890, 43 percent of Detroit's population was German.[18] "Germans basically controlled the city and its culture," said Bill Loomis, a Detroit food historian. "In the 1890s about a third of the houses in Detroit were owned by Germans." Naturally, someone had to feed them.

George Schweizer, an immigrant from Bavaria,[19] opened Schweizer's around 1862 on Hastings Street.[20] It was first listed as a grocery and then as a saloon, catering to the workers at the nearby rail yards, foundries, lumber mills and boarding houses. The food was the type to fill up the laborers, while also giving the Germans among them a taste of home. Sauerbraten and potato pancakes were popular, as was the weiner schnitzel—German 101 cuisine. As the years went on, the restaurant grew with the changing downtown neighborhood, offering banquet facilities and business luncheons, becoming famous for its sauerbraten as well as steaks and chops, expanding into three adjacent buildings, and eventually lending its name to the street it was on—Schweizer Place. "Run by the same family, it never blew out its lamps, even during the drear days of prohibition," wrote Frank Bury Woodford and Arthur M. Woodford in 1969,[21] acknowledging its continued existence for over 100 years at that point, though during prohibition it reverted to a grocery. It was neither an elite downtown spot like the London Chop House nor a scenic river resort—it was located right in the middle of those two spots, and too far from either to attract those crowds. Still, it survived for 130 years.

And yet somehow, despite its longevity and apparent fame, Schweizer's disappeared. In 1980 *Grosse Pointe News* ran an ad about an auction featuring paintings from Schweizer's. Some errant matchbooks and postcards can be found for sale. Its name is grouped with a dozen others to signify the city's "dining past," and yet that's where its legacy seems to end. Given that Detroit was so heavily German, how was it forgotten? How did over a century of German heritage vanish with barely a cry?

At the turn of the 20th century, "hyphenated American" was a derogatory term particularly targeted at German Americans. "Hyphenated Americans," instead of embracing both their home countries and their adopted ones, were seen as cowards or possible spies, especially when they called for neutrality in World War I. In 1915, President Theodore Roosevelt delivered a speech in New York City, saying, "There is no room in this country for hyphenated Americanism. . .a hyphenated American is not an American at all." The country was rife with anti-German sentiment (sauerkraut was even called "liberty cabbage," a nice precursor to "freedom fries"), and many of the country's Germans were quick to shed markers of their heritage. There were churches and businesses like Schweizer's that survived, but there was not a rally around that heritage that other ethnicities, like Polish or Irish, had and continue to celebrate in Detroit today.

In 1983 Schweizer's turned into another bar and grill and later into a nightclub, and in 2014 the building was demolished. The news reports that ran mentioned it had been the 130-year home of Schweizer's and left it at that. By that point, there was no one left to remember. Though about one in four people[22] in the metro Detroit area boast German roots, those who would have gone to Schweizer's in its heyday are long gone, and their descendants have moved away. But it accomplished the monumental task of keeping German heritage alive at a time when many wanted to abandon it. It's hard to erase something like that.

SCHWEIZER'S SAUERBRATEN

These two recipes were found handwritten in an attic in Hamtramck, Michigan by Michael Jackman, with the note "Schweizer's celebrating 100ᵗʰ Birthday this year," dating them to around 1962.[23] Legend has it that New York German restaurant Luchow's originated the trend of using gingersnaps to thicken the gravy for sauerbraten, a traditional pickled beef roast. Other recipes call for crumbled gingerbread or lebkuchen, so crushed gingersnaps surely get the job done, and whether or not Luchow's originated it, the idea made its way to Detroit. The sweetness cuts the flavorful vinegar brine, which pickles the meat for five days in the fridge. It's well worth the wait.

SERVES 4

4 lb (1.8 kg) beef bottom round

1 cup (236 ml) red wine vinegar

3 cups (710 ml) water

2 cloves garlic

2 onions, sliced

1 carrot, sliced

1 bay leaf

1 tbsp (15 g) pickling spice

Salt and pepper

3 tbsp (45 ml) corn oil

Flour

1 tsp (5 g) sugar

1 tomato, diced

4 to 5 gingersnaps, pulverized in a food processor

Schweizer's Potato Pancakes (page 31), optional

Cover the beef round in a mixture of the vinegar, water, garlic, onions, carrot, bay leaf, pickling spice, salt and pepper to taste. Marinate the meat for five days in the refrigerator. If the meat isn't fully submerged, rotate it every other day so it brines evenly.

Remove the meat from the marinade and pat it dry. Set the remaining marinade aside. Heat the oil in a Dutch oven over high heat. Dust the meat with flour and brown on all sides, about 2 to 3 minutes per side. Once browned, add the remaining marinade liquid with its vegetables, the sugar and tomato to the Dutch oven. Lower the heat and braise until the meat is tender, around 2½ to 3 hours. When done, strain the sauce left in the pan into a small saucepan over medium heat. Add the gingersnaps and cook until the gravy is thickened, about 5 to 7 minutes more. Salt and pepper to taste.

The sauerbraten should be served sliced thin, 5 or 6 slices per person, drizzled with the gravy and paired with potato pancakes if you'd like.

SCHWEIZER'S POTATO PANCAKES

This handwritten recipe for Schweizer's potato pancakes cautions to "never use a blender" when grating the potatoes, but the grater attachment on a food processor will work just fine. The crispy, fluffy pancakes make an excellent accompaniment to Schweizer's sauerbraten, or served on their own with sour cream or applesauce.

MAKES 8 PANCAKES, SERVES 4

4 medium-size potatoes, peeled

1 onion

3 eggs

1 tbsp (15 g) flour

1 tsp (5 g) baking powder

½ tsp salt

¼ cup (60 ml) corn oil

Grate or grind the potatoes and onion into a sieve. Squeeze to remove as much water as possible, then transfer to a bowl and gently mix with eggs, flour, baking powder and salt. Heat the corn oil over high heat in a large skillet, and slide a spoonful of batter gently into the hot oil, making sure to heap high for thick, fluffy pancakes. Turn once, when pancakes are a golden brown, after about 5 minutes. Let the pancakes drain on a paper towel, and serve alongside Sauerbraten (page 28) or on their own.

[23] For reference information see Endnotes.

LOCKE-OBER

Boston, MA
1875-2012

———·———

In 1970, Locke-Ober experimented with letting women into its main men's cafe in honor of Women's Liberation Day. On December 30 of that year, they decided it wasn't for them. "Men just don't want them, and real ladies don't want to intrude on a man's privacy," said Frank Carro,[24] the men's cafe's maitre d'. Horrified, he described how mothers came in with their children, attempting to order hot dogs and hamburgers, disrupting the way things were supposed to be run. "We can't allow Locke-Ober to be turned into a hash house after all these years of building up a fine reputation." That didn't last long; the restaurant admitted women again just the next year, and they certainly weren't the only stragglers to the equality table. But the anecdote is a bit representative of the kind of place Locke-Ober was. At that point, it had been around almost 100 years. No point in changing then.

Locke-Ober opened in 1875, and when it closed in 2012, it was the third-oldest restaurant in Boston. Its first owner, Louis Ober, had moved to America from Alsace, and combined a restaurant and a bar that had been operating next to each other on Winter Place to make Ober's Restaurant Parisien, which would be renamed. It advertised itself as serving exclusively French food, though as time went on, that would expand to cater to New England's seafood palate. However, the point was as much the atmosphere as it was the food. The *Boston Globe* described it as Boston's "queen dowager, dressed in finery, eating off only the best linen and china, and drinking imported tea with her pinky finger extended."[25]

Naturally, the Kennedys went there, as did visiting dignitaries, politicians and power brokers, getting high on Locke-Ober's borrowed opulence. "It had a grandness about it that very few American places have," said Brad Haskel, who worked there in the late 1980s. "Time stood still in Locke-Ober . . . You walked into a different time period." And for many years, it could survive on just that. Boston is known for many things, but until recently, a vibrant and adventurous restaurant scene was not one of them.

The story Locke-Ober told about itself was that it was Boston's stalwart restaurant, beautiful and grand and important, the kind of place that would always be there. It's a story lots of restaurants buy into, but "always" is never a guarantee, and things were changing. Americans were increasingly interested in different types of cuisines. Women were increasingly gaining access to places where they had long been denied. Boston was no longer a culinary backwater. Downtown Crossing was turning into an undesirable neighborhood. Some changes were for the best and some weren't, and Locke-Ober found itself caught between wanting to honor its past, and catering to a very different Boston than the one in which it had been founded.

The restaurant fought for a long time. In 2001 Chef Lydia Shire came on as its first female chef, attempting to update its menu while keeping true to its history, but by the time it closed no middle ground could be found. The older generations thought it had changed too much, and the younger ones thought it hadn't changed enough, and whether the economy, the location or increased competition was to blame, it never found the right balance that could move it into the next generation.

Most people would not trade the equality of the sexes for the sake of "tradition," but when Locke-Ober went, so did some traditions that may have been worth keeping around. "There was a rich history with the people in the back of a house," said Haskel. "There was a long history of people who had stayed there," including the chef during Haskel's time, who had worked his way up from being a dishwasher, back when being a chef was a far less glamorous position. "It was a different mentality," said Haskel, and one that has largely disappeared, for better or for worse.

Locke-Ober's Finnan Haddie Delmonico

According to the New York Times, *"finnan haddie," also known as cold-smoked haddock, was popular among early American settlers, especially in New England, where it was served poached in milk with lots of butter. This elevated version of finnan haddie stays true to those New England roots, while adding a few restaurant-quality spins, like the elegant piped potato border, and a sprinkling of Parmesan. This is a perfect use of any leftover mashed potatoes you may have laying around.*

Serves 4

1½ lb (680 g) cold-smoked haddock (finnan haddie)

¼ cup (57 g) butter

3 tbsp (24 g) flour

2 cups (473 ml) cream

4 hard-boiled eggs, quartered

Salt and pepper to taste

Mashed potatoes

Grated Parmesan cheese

Preheat the oven to 400°F (204°C). Place the fish in a shallow pan and barely cover with water. Cover and simmer for 15 minutes. Drain and let cool, and then bone the fish and flake into good-size pieces.

Melt the butter in a double boiler and whisk in the flour. Slowly add cream, whisking constantly. Continue to whisk until the sauce comes to a boil. Let boil for 2 minutes.

Add the fish and the eggs to the cream sauce, folding carefully to avoid breaking up the fish. Add salt and pepper to taste, and pour the mixture into a 9 x 9-inch (22.8 x 22.8-cm) baking dish. Pipe a border of mashed potatoes around the dish using a pastry tube. Sprinkle the top generously with Parmesan cheese. Bake until top is golden brown, about 10 minutes.

[26] For reference information see Endnotes.

LOCKE-OBER'S BAKED LOBSTER SAVANNAH

This decadent baked lobster—the meat baked in its own shell and topped with crispy breadcrumbs and cheese—is what Locke-Ober was all about: distinctly New England flavors, and an extravagant recipe that stands the test of time.

SERVES 2

NEWBURG SAUCE

1 tbsp (15 g) butter

¼ tsp Spanish paprika

1½ tbsp (12 g) flour

1 cup (236 ml) milk

Salt to taste

⅛ tsp white pepper

1 tbsp (15 ml) dry sherry

1 (3 lb [1.3 kg]) live lobster

1 tbsp (15 g) butter, melted

¼ tsp salt

1 cup (236 ml) standard Newburg sauce

½ cup (120 g) mushrooms, chopped

¼ cup (60 g) green peppers, diced

1 tsp (5 g) paprika

1 red pimiento, sliced

Salt and pepper to taste

¼ cup (60 g) breadcrumbs

¼ cup (60 g) Parmesan cheese, grated

Sherry wine and lemon juice to garnish

To make Newburg sauce, melt the butter in a large skillet. Add the paprika and stir well, then gradually add the flour to make a roux. In a separate saucepan, scald the milk, and then gradually whisk into the roux. Cook, stirring constantly, until thickened, about 5 minutes. Season with salt and pepper and add the sherry. Let simmer for a few more minutes, then remove from heat and strain. This should make about a cup (230 g) of sauce.

Preheat oven to 375°F (190°C). Bring a pot of salted water to a boil. Once boiling, plunge the lobster into the pot, cover and boil for half an hour. Remove and let cool, then remove the claws and legs from the lobster. Using kitchen shears, neatly cut an oval opening from the top of the head to the tail, and remove meat from the body and claws. Save the lobster shell for stuffing later. Cut the lobster meat into cubes and place in a buttered baking pan with melted butter and salt. Bake for 20 minutes, then remove and drain the excess liquid. Add the lobster meat to a pan with Newburg sauce, mushrooms and green peppers, and cook over low heat, stirring occasionally, for 15 minutes. Remove from heat and stir in paprika and pimiento.

Season the filling with salt and pepper, then pile it into the lobster shell. Mix the breadcrumbs and cheese and sprinkle on top, then bake for 15 minutes, until the top is golden brown. Remove from oven, sprinkle with sherry and lemon juice, and serve.

[27] For reference information see Endnotes.

THOMPSON'S SPA

Boston, MA

1882-1968

⸻·⸻

The soda we know today is not the soda of the mid-19th century. Now it's bottled and high-fructose corn syrup laden, pre-mixed and dispensed by machines. Then, it was the new frontier in health. Temperance movements were growing, with activists and politicians calling for alternatives and solutions to what was functionally America's widespread drinking problem (in 1830, the average American drank 3.9 gallons [15 L] of alcohol per year).[28] Many also associated sparkling waters with restorative properties, and in the 1830s, Sarasota Springs, New York, became one of the most popular vacation spots in the country as tourists indulged in their mineral springs. The time was right for the drugstore soda fountain, and Thompson's Spa became known as one of the best.

Charles Eaton opened the first location of Thompson's Spa, named specifically to evoke the health associations of mineral waters, in 1882, ironically on the same street as Boston's first licensed ordinary, Cole's Inn.[29] At first he sold nothing but "temperance drinks," such as egg phosphates, sodas and lemonades. Previously, these types of drinks were the province of drugstores, since they were believed to be medicinal. Druggists would add medicines to flavored sodas to make them easier to take (and back when cocaine, radium and heroin were considered medicines), and they often provided a quick fix for those who needed it when the taverns were closed. As the *Brooklyn Daily Eagle* put it in 1886, "There is still another class of people, the members of which, averse to being seen in a legitimate drinking place, take their toddy under the guise of a tonic, or veiled beneath the foaming crest of the soda chalice."[30]

That may have been the case at the drugstore, but places like Thompson's were created specifically as temperance saloons, offering all of the social benefits and theatricality of a tavern without the buzz. "I am convinced that the drinking of light wines or beers undoubtedly creates an appetite for stronger liquors," Eaton told the *American Magazine of Civics* in 1895, and that "temperance would be advanced by encouraging places for the sale of non-alcoholic drinks, and, if possible, by making the opportunity socially prominent."[31] It was certainly going that way; in 1895 Thompson's Spa made $50,000, and there were over 100,000 soda fountains in America.[32]

In 1895 an egg phosphate at Thompson's cost ten cents, and Eaton began serving pies and sandwiches to please the lunch crowd. The spa was located in "Newspaper Row," a district home to many of Boston's papers, which is perhaps why Thompson's had such an easy time with publicity. Reporters, politicians, lawyers and more would gather at Thompson's for lunch, and the *Boston Globe* reported the daily weather by consulting the thermometer built on the restaurant's exterior. Soon, it was one of the most famous spas in America, and by the 1920s it was a publicly traded company with multiple locations across Massachusetts,[33] and soda experts from around the country would go to Thompson's to try their sodas, which were served from automated pipes and machines that Eaton, a graduate of MIT, designed himself.

Part of Thompson's appeal was simply quantity—there were over 160 drink options, all designed by Eaton himself before his death in 1917. However, it was also about ease, and some pseudo-science. A phosphate or soda often contained eggs, ginger or other nutritious ingredients, meaning "many a tired man too weary and jaded to eat anything solid or substantial in the way of a luncheon, can manage to swallow an 'egg lemonade' or a 'milk shake' or both," according to Jean Kinkaid in the *Boston Daily Globe* in 1889.[34] Thus, a man can get the nutrients he needs, with "little demand on his digestive organs." It was a selling point that these were easy to digest, and Kinkaid argued that sipping these concoctions meant "the stomach has much less labor to perform in heating it up to the necessary temperature, while the dangers to the gastric nerves and solar plexus are much lessened." At any rate, "if it were not for the 'temperance bar' and its hygienic drinks, this man would have gone without lunch."

Over the years, the soda fountain evolved. Thompson's changed from a quick stop at a counter (where only men were allowed) to a full-service restaurant, while soda turned from something crafted for you by an expert soda jerk to something to get out of a bottle from a Coca-Cola machine. By the 1940s and '50s, soda was still popular, but it no longer held its curative allure, and no longer had to be found at the fountain. Internal issues plagued Thompson's as well, from family arguments to a strike, and by 1968 the last lunchroom had closed.

In 2013, Americans drank on average 44 gallons (176 L) of soda a year, and links to obesity and diabetes have made large-scale, enthusiastic consumption of soda somewhat of a taboo, just as alcohol was when the soda fountain began to rise. Thompson's Spa may not have been able to get away with their sales pitch today, but then again, Mountain Dew is nothing compared to an expertly made egg phosphate.

THOMPSON'S SPA EGG PHOSPHATE

A classic soda counter drink, Thompson's egg phosphate was considered one of the best in the country, its soda jerks experts in their field. The egg gives body to what otherwise would be fizzy lemonade. You can see how this would have been considered a fortifying, refreshing drink to get you through the afternoon. If you really want to be authentic, pair it with a ham sandwich.

MAKES 2 DRINKS

½ cup (226 g) sugar

7 lemons, divided

1 egg, beaten

½ oz (14 ml) acid phosphate

Ice

Soda water

To make the lemon syrup, combine sugar and the zest of three lemons in a small saucepan. Add ½ cup (118 ml) of water, and boil until the sugar is dissolved and the syrup is clear. Remove from heat, and add the juice of 6 lemons. Let cool, then strain.

To make the egg phosphates, combine the egg, 1 ounce (28 ml) lemon syrup, 1 ounce (28 ml) lemon juice, acid phosphate and ½ ounce (14 ml) water in a shaker over ice. Shake until combined and cold, then strain into two Collins glasses. Fill each glass the rest of the way with soda water.

[35] For reference information see Endnotes.

WOLF'S ROADHOUSE

Windsor, Canada
1887-1920s

————·——

"Now, you tak nice, fat bullfrog, an cut off hees hin' laig. Skin heem, soak heem in salt water, an' parboil heem. Den you roll heem in corn meal—or mebbe you lak de fine cracker crumb. After dat you fry heem brown in buttaire, an'—an'—I jes 'zactly soon have chicken!"

According to the *New York Times*,[36] this recipe comes from a French Canadian frog trapper, who in 1927 could reportedly earn around $50,000 a year. By that time, frog legs were popular in large hotels across America, but before the rest of the country got a taste for them, there was one place where they were always on the menu—Detroit roadhouses.

Detroit food historian Bill Loomis says the roadhouse was a uniquely Detroit kind of place. "They were resorts built right along the Detroit River, on both the American and Canadian sides. A lot of them were owned by Germans or French Canadians." On weekends families would escape the city by heading up to the river. The roadhouse served chicken or fresh fried fish, but they also were famous for serving local delicacies like muskrat and frog legs.

Wolf's Roadhouse, founded in 1887 just on the other side of the river from Detroit in Windsor, Ontario, was one of the most popular roadhouses in the area. It was run by Wolfgang Feller, a German immigrant who made his name as a hunter and local guide, and bought the hotel and surrounding 85-acre farm. He used Peche Island in the Detroit river as his fishery, kept ducks on a canal beside the road, and once made a dinner of muskrat he discovered stealing liquor from his storage room. Soon, it became "the most famous roadhouse in [that] part of the country."[37]

In 1927, as America's prohibition raged on, Canada's prohibition act expired, leaving it up to the individual provinces as to whether to continue the ban. Ontario did, but Windsor became a hotbed of rum-running and organized crime as liquor was smuggled across the American border. The *New York Times*[38] picked up Wolfgang Feller's obituary in 1931, and mentioned that, after forty years, Wolf's closed when "licenses were revoked on the advent of prohibition." A frog trapper may have been able to earn a lot of money, but frogs weren't worth much to an innkeeper with a liquor license lost in a legal scuffle.

Feller's obituary also noted that Wolf's, in its day, "was famous as an epicurian's paradise," perhaps because of the way it melded its influences. It was a place where a German immigrant could serve French Canadian dishes, where Americans could spend a leisurely afternoon in Canada, and where a unique culinary tradition could thrive. It may have been in Canada, but it was distinctly Detroit.

WOLF'S ROADHOUSE FRIED FROG LEGS

These are the kind of frog legs served at nearly every Detroit roadhouse, and later in fancier restaurants and hotels as "roadhouse style." When that French Canadian trapper said, "I jes 'zactly soon have chicken," he was onto something—the flavor of frog is quite similar, slightly lighter and chewier, but extremely moist. It was popular to coat them in cracker crumbs instead of flour at the time.

SERVES 4

---

1 lb (453 g) frog legs

10 soda crackers

Salt and pepper

4 tbsp (57 g) butter, plus more for dipping

Soak the frog legs in heavily salted water for half an hour. Bring a small pot of water to a boil, then drop frog legs in and boil for three minutes. Remove from water and pat dry with a towel.

In a food processor, grind the crackers until fine, or use a rolling pin. Mix with salt and pepper to taste, and lay on a plate. Roll the frog legs in the cracker crumbs until fully coated. Heat the butter in a skillet over medium high heat, and pan-fry the frog legs until golden brown on each side and meat has cooked through, about 5 minutes per side. Serve with more melted butter for dipping.

Old Original Bookbinder's/ Bookbinder's Seafood House

Philadelphia, PA

1890s–2009

———

The history of Old Original Bookbinder's in Philadelphia isn't really the history of Old Original Bookbinder's, mainly because what constitutes "original" isn't quite clear. Is it the location that counts, or the people running it? The history of Old Original Bookbinder's is really the history of both the Bookbinder family and the two restaurants that shared their name, spun off from each other due to a family feud.

Samuel Bookbinder was a Jewish immigrant from Holland who arrived in Philadelphia around 1880. "He lived near 5th street and South street," said Connie Bookbinder, whose husband remained in the family business. "That's where the ships would come in on the wharf. At first he'd put out water for the sailors, then he put out a big pot of soup and charged them for it." When that became successful, he opened a restaurant at 125 Walnut Street, taking over Beyer's Restaurant, another oyster house. Soon after the business changed hands, previous owner Attila Beyer skipped town, leaving behind some unpaid loans.

The restaurant was immensely popular, attracting sailors and townsfolk alike with dishes like Snapper Soup (page 51) and fresh lobster. The restaurant was eventually taken over by Samuel's son, Emanuel, who continued to expand it into adjacent buildings. He also spent some time in prison after $50,000 worth of liquor was seized from the restaurant in 1921—"reported to be the biggest cache ever seized under the Volstead Act"[39] at the time. He wound up serving over eight months at Mercer County Jail in Trenton, only to be raided again in 1925 when police broke up a "wild party" taking place at the restaurant.[40]

In the 1930s, the family rift began. After Emanuel died the restaurant passed to his sister, Hattie, who hired her nephew, Samuel Bookbinder II (nicknamed Murph). "Auntie says to Murph, 'you're not going to work for me and run around with the waitresses!'" after she found out he had fallen in love with another member of the staff. Murph quit and opened his own restaurant, Bookbinder's Seafood House, on 15th street in 1934. Hattie died a few years later and her husband, Harmon Blackburn, donated Old Original Bookbinder's to the Federation of Jewish Charities in 1945 in her honor (and because, it being WW II, he couldn't find anyone to run it). In turn, they sold it to John Taxin, whose family continued to run the restaurant until it closed in 2002. But for nearly 70 years there were two Bookbinder's in Philadelphia, and it led to some confusion. "Taxin hired a PR director, who says you can't have two restaurants calling themselves the same thing, and since this building was here first, they'll call it Old Original Bookbinder's, so people will want to go to the 'real' one." Bookbinder's Seafood House did its best to assert its authenticity. The bottom of their menu in 1941 reminded customers that they had "no other connection with any other restaurant bearing a similar name."[41]

At both locations, the family was known for seafood, especially lobster. Lobster Coleman (page 47), which used another family name, was a popular dish, as well as their many seafood soups and their famous Hot Slaw (page 48). It served quality seafood that, on occasion, hinted at its humbler beginnings. They were as happy to serve an elaborate Lobster Thermidor as they were a classic seafood stew. According to Connie, people came to Bookbinder's Seafood House for the service, especially once they realized the original Bookbinder family was running it. "When you walked in, you were met by Mr. Bookbinder, and the customers used to ask him to autograph the menu so they could take it with them." Murph seemed a natural restaurateur, quite a feat considering he had been deaf since he was 16. He learned to read lips expertly, and would get the cashiers to repeat phone calls to him so he could see what they were saying and respond. Almost no one was the wiser.

The two restaurants had a friendly enough relationship. "They almost have to cooperate in self-preservation, given the intensely competitive explosion of eating places that in the last 10 to 15 years has earned Philadelphia a reputation as an exciting restaurant town," wrote the *New York Times*[42] in 1985, describing just how often a dinner party would find themselves split between the two, each side assuming they were at the "right" one. And not only was Philadelphia becoming a dining destination in the 1980s and 1990s, most customers didn't know the elaborate backstory as to how there came to be two Bookbinder's, and would naturally associate them with one another. "The Taxins franchised it for a while," said Connie, "There was an Old Original Bookbinder's in Virginia. We went there one night and were pleased to see they were doing a lovely job with our name. Because we're the ones who get blamed!"

Though it lacked the "Old Original" name, locals and celebrities alike appreciated the family-run Bookbinder's Seafood House. Everyone from Liberace to Bob Hope was a regular, and anyone with a Bookbinder name in the Philadelphia area became a local celebrity. But as Connie and her husband, Samuel Bookbinder III, got older, they realized they no longer wanted to be in the restaurant business. "There are so many restaurants that were so wonderful that are gone, and it's so sad because many have been replaced with restaurants that are chains," she said. Ironic, as Bookbinder's Seafood House was replaced by an Applebee's.[43] Old Original Bookbinder's closed in 2009, ending a more-than-100-year residency of Bookbinder seafood in Philadelphia. The name, whomever it belonged to, stood for a long time.

Bookbinder's Lobster Coleman

Few things seem as extravagant as stuffed lobster, especially when one uses more than one type of meat. The mixture of lobster and crab needs little else to shine, which is why this classic dish remained popular throughout Bookbinder's Seafood House's life.

SERVES 2

1 (2–3 lb [907 g–1.3 kg]) lobster, split

3 tbsp (45 ml) melted butter, divided

Salt and pepper to taste

1 tsp (5 g) parsley, minced

½ lb (226 g) fresh crabmeat

Dash of paprika

Split the lobster down the middle lengthwise, being sure not to cut all the way through (you can have your fishmonger do this). Lay the lobster open as far as possible and pull out and discard the dark vein running from tail to stomach (in the head), and the stomach and spongy substances inside. You can save the green liver and red coral for decoration or seasoning if you wish.

Place the lobster top shell side up on broiler rack 3 inches (7.6 cm) from heat. Brush with 2 tablespoons (30 ml) melted butter (or the green liver mixed with melted butter), salt, pepper and minced parsley. Broil for 8 minutes under medium heat. Remove the lobster from the broiler, and once cool enough to handle, remove the meat from body of the lobster, keeping the shell intact. Chop or cut the lobster meat and combine it with the fresh crabmeat, and stuff it back into body of the lobster.

Brush the filling with remaining melted butter and a dash of paprika, then broil for 5 to 7 minutes or until tender, brushing often with melted seasoned butter while broiling. Serve at once.

[44] For reference information see Endnotes.

BOOKBINDER'S—121-23-25 Walnut Street, Philadelphia, Pa.

BOOKBINDER'S—Famous for Sea Foods from Coast to Coast

BOOKBINDER'S HOT SLAW

According to Connie Bookbinder, this slaw with a ketchup-based dressing was unique to Bookbinder's, and a good alternative for all those averse to mayonnaise-based slaws. No, it is neither hot in temperature nor flavor, but who's counting?

SERVES 4

1 cup (236 ml) ketchup

1¼ cups (250 g) sugar

¾ cup (177 ml) white vinegar

1½ cups (354 ml) vegetable oil

¾ cup (177 ml) lemon juice

1½ tsp (7.5 g) paprika

Salt and pepper to taste

1 head green cabbage, shredded

Whisk together the ketchup, sugar, vinegar, oil, lemon juice, paprika, salt and pepper. Pour over shredded cabbage and toss until fully incorporated.

[45] For reference information see Endnotes.

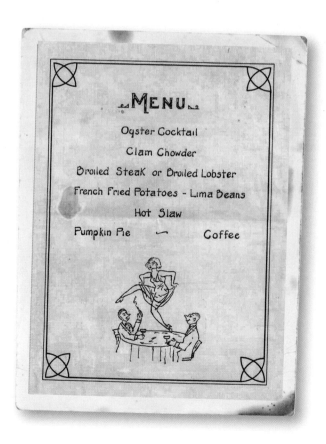

Bookbinder's Snapper Soup

This soup ("laced with sherry") was the prize dish of Bookbinder's, and is like nothing I've ever tasted, probably because it uses nearly every spice in the spice rack. A few recipes are floating around that offer close approximations, but this one comes from the notes used in the Bookbinder's kitchen, scaled down so as not to laden anyone with 100 servings of soup. Turtle meat can still be found in some specialty seafood and game shops, but veal and turkey make completely acceptable substitutes.

SERVES 6

STOCK

½ lb (226 g) freshwater turtle meat, dark turkey meat or veal shank

1 lemon

¼ cup (60 g) pickling spice

1 bay leaf

2 cloves garlic

SOUP

2 tbsp (30 g) butter

1 large onion, finely chopped

3 stalks celery, finely chopped

2 cloves garlic, chopped

1½ tbsp (22.5 g) beef base

1 tbsp (15 g) chicken base

2 tbsp (30 g) paprika

1 tbsp (15 g) garlic powder

1 tbsp (15 g) dry mustard

1 tbsp (15 g) onion powder

¼ tsp nutmeg

½ tsp mace

½ tsp allspice

½ tsp celery salt

½ tsp ground cloves

½ tsp marjoram

½ tsp thyme

½ tsp oregano

½ tsp basil

¼ tsp cayenne

1 cup (128 g) flour

3 oz (88 ml) sherry

½ oz (15 ml) Worcestershire sauce

1 oz (30 ml) A1 Sauce

1 tbsp (15 g) sugar

3 hard-boiled eggs, chopped

Salt to taste

To make the stock, cover the meat, lemon, pickling spice, bay leaf and garlic with 6 cups (1.4 L) of water. Bring to a boil, and then simmer for about 45 minutes, until the meat is cooked through. Remove the meat from the stock and coarsely chop. Set aside. Strain the rest of the stock into a large bowl and set aside. (This can be done a day in advance.)

In a large stockpot, melt the butter over low heat, and add the onion, celery and garlic. Cook until onions are translucent, about 10 minutes, then slowly whisk in the beef base and chicken base. Add the rest of the dry spices and whisk together for another minute. Slowly whisk in the stock and the flour, about a cup each at a time, until all the ingredients are fully incorporated and there are no lumps. Raise the heat to bring the soup to a boil, then lower and simmer for about half an hour. Add the sherry, Worcestershire sauce, A1 sauce and sugar and simmer for another 10 minutes, then add eggs and meat. Check for salt and serve.

[46] For reference information see Endnotes.

ERNST CAFÉ

New Orleans, LA
Opened 1902

New Orleans clings to its restaurant history. Restaurants like Commander's Palace, Galatoire's and Antoine's do not slip away because of changing tastes and rent hikes, but calcify around their own legacies, serving their signatures a century down the line. When restaurants do go they go violently, through death or destruction, almost always against the city's will. In the case of Ernst Café, even a twelve-year closure wasn't enough to be a nail in the coffin. Family tradition outweighed all.

In 1900, William Ernst, the son of two German immigrants, had been operating a bar and pool room at 600 South Peters Street, in a warehouse that was built in the 1850s. The bar catered to the blue-collar dock workers and manufacturers working in the area, many of whom were from German, Irish or Italian descent. William's brother, Charles Ernst, bought the bar from him that year and in 1902 opened Ernst Café. "Café" is a bit of a misleading term—it was more of a saloon, where beer was served for a nickel and came with a free lunch of sandwiches or sardines.[47] The bar was built by Brunswick, the same company that made pool tables, which had a cabinet shop set up in nearby Jax Brewery. "They would give you a complete bar and build it in in place in return for an exclusive sale of their product," explained Lou Tortorich, Ernst's great-grandson, who would eventually take over the bar.

There was another interesting feature to the bar—a mosaic floor whose pattern greatly resembled a swastika. The floor was there long before Hitler's rise to power, and Tortorich said it's actually an "ancient American Indian symbol for peace," inspired by the Tchopitoulas tribe who used to live by the river. Similar patterns were certainly used by Southern American Indian tribes, and many other civilizations, but plenty of people began to notice. "Back when my grandfather was there, Jewish people would come in and know instantly what it was."

Around 1930 Charles Ernst's son, Malcolm, took over operations and expanded the food options, serving what would come to be classic New Orleans cuisine—po' boys, gumbo, red beans and rice, and "always fried seafood." The location ensured a steady stream of customers, but by the 1960s things were changing. "That neighborhood was run down, and there were dilapidated warehouses around," said Tortorich. "The majority of my grandparents' business back then were the longshoremen off the riverfront. They served 25-cent po' boys." Now the shipping and manufacturing industries were going away, but there was nothing to replace them. In 1969 the café closed, and the building leased to a woman who had run a "colored restaurant" behind Ernst Café.

In many cities, that's where the story would end. The neighborhood changed, business got tough, and the restaurant was replaced by one catering to a new community. But in New Orleans the past never quite disappears. In 1980 the Ernsts were attempting to sell the building, but their grandsons Lou Tortorich and his brother Wayne realized the cafe could have a second chance. "I grew up at Ernst," said Tortorich, and the brothers were no strangers to New Orleans restaurant culture—their other great-grandfather founded the French Quarter stalwart Tortorici's, which only closed after Hurricane Katrina. Initially they encouraged their grandparents to sell the building, but by 1981 they realized that in a few short years, the World's Fair would be coming to New Orleans. The listing expired, and the brothers got to work rebuilding the bar, and reopened just in time for the 1984 World's Fair.

"All suits and ties," Tortorich said of the new clientele to *Dixie*[48] in 1983. "They come between 7 and 8 at night, have a couple of drinks and go home. I couldn't ask for a better clientele." It was certainly a far cry from the longshoremen, and now the office buildings, hotels and convention centers of the Central Business District (what the warehouses have been renamed) only guarantee more well-off customers. But if there's one thing the longshoremen and the businessmen had in common, it was an appreciation of the food. It seems nobody could resist a good gumbo.

Tortorich sold Ernst Café in 2000, and the new owners are required to maintain the name and history of the restaurant, something that continues to be valued. "The restaurants that are still around and were taken over, were taken over by people who still had the same ethics and personality as the family," he said. "It's not necessarily about the continuation of the family, but the continuation of the history." Lucky for them they're in New Orleans, where history is rarely forgotten.

Ernst Café Shrimp Stew

This simple stew has all the flavor you'd expect from a New Orleans seafood dish, and you can dial up the red pepper if you're looking for something hotter. Serve it with a beer and lots of bread to soak up what's left in the bowl.

Serves 6-8

8 tbsp (113 g) of butter

1 cup (240 g) bell pepper, diced

1 small onion, diced

1 tsp (5 g) salt

1 tsp (5 g) red pepper

1 tsp (5 g) dried oregano

1 (32-oz [907-g]) can tomato sauce

¼ cup (50 g) sugar

2 tsp (10 g) dried parsley

2 lb (907 g) carrots, diced

2 lb (907 g) potatoes, diced

4 lb (1.8 kg) shrimp, peeled

Melt the butter in the bottom of a large pot over low heat. Add the bell pepper, onion, salt, red pepper and oregano, and sauté until the onion is translucent but the rest of the vegetables remain fairly crisp, about 10 minutes. Add the tomato sauce, sugar, parsley, carrots and potatoes, and cook together for a minute. Add water until the pot is three-quarters full, then cover and simmer for about 30 minutes, stirring often to prevent sticking, until carrots are tender. Add shrimp, cover again and simmer for another 5 minutes, then turn off heat and let stand for 45 minutes before serving.

[332] For reference information see Endnotes.

OVERLAND HOTEL

Gardnerville, NV
1900s-2014

————·————

America's immigrants have often relied on community centers and organizations run by their fellow country-men for support and guidance. It's a way to find commonality in a new environment, a way to keep traditions and customs alive, and in the best of cases, introduce them to others. For the Basque population that settled in the American west in the mid-1800s, these establishments were known as *ostatu*, and the Overland Hotel was a classic example of an immigrant outpost that supported Basque immigrants. "Nevada has a proud Basque history," said Nevada Senator Dean Heller,[49] "and the Overland Hotel embodies that long and rich tradition."

Ostatu are essentially boarding houses that feature a bar and restaurant for both boarders and anyone passing by. They began popping up in California, Nevada and other western states in the 1860s,[50] as Basques, some of whom had already fled to the Americas due to poverty, came to participate in the gold rush and subsequently turned to steadier and more familiar work shepherding and ranching. Initially, these boarding houses were by Basques and for Basques, rarely serving to outside patrons. According to the Juansara family, who operated the Overland Hotel in the 1953, Basque herders could come and stay between seasons herding in California and looking for jobs further south in the winter. However, the ostatu operated not just as boarding houses, but support centers. It was not uncommon for proprietors to help herders with immigration papers, banking and finding seasonal work.

The Overland Hotel was constructed in Gardnerville, Nevada, in the early 1900s (there are conflicting dates), on America's first transcontinental highway. It wasn't a Basque ostatu then, but rather a meat market.[51] In 1921 Basque immigrant John Etchemendy, a former shepherd, became a partner[52] and turned it into a hotel with a bar and restaurant. Over the years it would be leased by a few families, including the Juansara family, who said in an interview in the 1980s[53] that they charged $3 a day for room and board for herders, which came with three meals, served family style across big tables. However, Basque immigration tapered at the beginning of the 20th century and many of the existing herders died or settled down. This led to ostatu opening their kitchens to the public. According to Nancy Zubiri, author of *A Travel Guide to Basque America: Families, Feasts, and Festivals*, it began with shepherds who had lived at these boardinghouses and would return with their families to eat occasionally, as she and her family did at the boardinghouse her father had lived in in San Francisco. "We would go back to the hotel on Sunday nights and eat there," she said. "Or Basques would bring their friends. Outsiders would come in to eat and pay for dinner, and they realized there was a business there."

The Overland Hotel was one of many Basque boardinghouses in Gardnerville that have become known for their simple, meat-heavy food. "It wasn't really Spanish or French Basque, but the food they were familiar with at home," says Zubiri. "This was country food. Big servings for people who work hard." They were known for their steak and lamb chops, but according to Mrs. Juansara they served much more than that. "Then sometimes I had roast pork or roast beef, or spare ribs" she said, along with soup, salad, a daily stew of everything from oxtail to offal, and sometimes up to a dozen dishes served family style, many heavy with garlic. Quantity has always been a hallmark. "To go to a Basque restaurant today you have to have an appetite, otherwise you'll waste the food."

Though there were still some herders left, by the 1950s the Juansaras admit they had more tourists staying and dining at the Overland than Basques. In the 1960s, it was even the venue for the American Legion Auxiliary to host a dinner, where the department president gave a speech on "Americanism."[54] The hotel changed hands again, and by 1967 was leased by Eusebio Cenoz, who owned it outright by 1976. Cenoz worked as a shepherd for twelve years after moving to America, and planned on making some money before moving back to Spain. However, he came to prefer the lifestyle he found in America. He quit shepherding once he felt he was too old for it, then worked at J&T bar and hotel, another Basque establishment in Gardnerville, before beginning to operate the Overland. "I cooked myself," he told an interviewer in 1988.[55] In 1980 he married his wife Elvira, who helped in the kitchen, and who continued managing the Overland herself after Eusebio died in 1989. "She was known for her lamb shanks," said Zubiri.

The Overland remained popular with locals and tourists alike, even as the Basque population and the establishments they frequented, began to disappear. Basque chefs are now better known for their Michelin-starred restaurants at the forefront of modernist cuisine, but the country cooking brought to America is harder to find. By the mid-2000s the Overland had just one Basque resident, and in 2014 Elvira decided it was time to retire. If you went to Gardnerville, you'd still see the old sign for the Overland, now adorning an American-style pub that took over the space but kept the name as an homage to the town's history. The Basque influence has become just that—history—and if you didn't know it was there you may not see it at all.

PICON PUNCH

The Picon Punch is the signature drink of the Basque boarding house. Picon is a bitter aperitif, popular in the Basque region of France, and the cocktail seems to be a distinctly Basque-American creation. Longtime Overland bartender Jesus Rey told the Record-Courier *that his secret is using "very little grenadine,"[56] so the bitter Picon really stands out.*

MAKES 1 DRINK

2 oz (60 ml) Picon (Torani Amer)

A dash soda water

½ oz (14 ml) grenadine

Ice

½ oz (14 ml) brandy

Lemon twist

Stir Picon, soda water and grenadine in a lowball glass over ice. Top with a float of brandy and a lemon twist.

HORN & HARDART'S AUTOMAT

Philadelphia, PA

1902-1991

In 1937 a reporter from the *New Yorker* who attended a gathering of Les Amis D'Escoffier was surprised to find Chef Bourdon of Horn & Hardart's Automat among the prestigious guests. Surely the purveyor of nickel coffee and pie that comes from a door in a wall wouldn't be considered among the country's culinary elite. The other guests, however, were not surprised at all; G. Selmer Fougner, wine columnist for the *Sun*, explained "the food in the Automats is simple but is impeccably prepared and highly regarded within the craft."[57] The sentiment was echoed by Anne Crawford Storz, who wrote to the *New York Times* about visiting her glamorous aunt in the city, and her mother's puzzlement that they'd always go to the Automat. When asked why they didn't go elsewhere, her aunt replied "Why indeed? The Automat has the best food in New York City. Why else?"[58]

Though heavily associated with New York, the Horn & Hardart Automat was actually a Philadelphia creation. Or was it New Orleans? Or Berlin? The story goes that Frank Hardart, a German-born, New Orleans–raised busboy, got the notion that New Orleans–style coffee would be a hit up north. He went to Philadelphia, where he found businessman John Horn, and in 1888 they opened their first coffee counter together. In 1900 Horn traveled to Berlin, where he discovered the Quisisana Company Automat. He bought their equipment, and had their chief engineer, John Fritsche, refine it further. They certainly weren't the first to experiment with automating food production, but H&H soon became known as "The Automat," the only place most associated with this type of technology.

The first Horn & Hardart Automat opened in Philadelphia in 1902. By 1912 there was one in New York, and at the height of their popularity post WW II they had over 80 locations in both cities, as well as a few waitress-service restaurants. Most of the food was made in two central commissaries (one in Philadelphia and one in New York) and driven to the locations around each city. The food was classic Americana—macaroni and cheese, baked beans and steak sandwiches were favorites, as well as the numerous pies and puddings. It was food that was quickly comforting, something that could be eaten on a lunch break, washed down with a cup of their impeccable coffee. In another remembrance to the *Times*,[59] Carol Lowenstein of Bayside, Queens, wrote of "people pouring free ketchup into glasses of free water and drinking a Depression cocktail." It was also an important asset for the growing population of working, single women, enabling them to dine alone and experience that public anonymity cities are so good for, without worry of judgmental stares or flirtations from waiters.

By the 1960s, H&H Automats were in decline—America had discovered faster food that they didn't even need to leave their cars to get. By 1971, the number of unprofitable locations outnumbered the profitable ones.[60] Already H&H had been attempting to get into the frozen food and institutional commissary businesses, publishing some recipes in advertorial campaigns alongside a line of frozen TV dinners. The few recipes Horn & Hardart did publish were drastically changed from their "in-house" recipes, scaled down from the commissary portions but often featuring completely different ingredients. However, Augustin S. Hardart Sr., former vice president of Horn & Hardart, kept a collection of the originals, including ones for 200 servings of baked beans or 20 gallons of salad dressing.

In 1991 the last H&H Automat, located on 42nd Street in Manhattan, closed its doors, a relic of a period in between a home-cooked meal and fast food.

HORN & HARDART'S BAKED BEANS

In the 1960s, the Automat published a few recipes in conjunction with its short-lived frozen food business. However, many of them featured entirely different ingredients and instructions than the recipes used in the cafeterias, as they had to be reimagined for the average home kitchen. This recipe for their famous baked beans comes not from the frozen-food recipe, but from the personal collection of Augustin S. Hardart. With mustard, brown butter and bacon, these baked beans avoid becoming the soupy, cloying dish many associate with the name, and instead come out savory and tangy with a hint of sweetness, made all the better topped with bacon. Originally, the recipe called for 50 pounds (22 kg) of beans, which would result in 197 servings. It's been scaled down considerably.

SERVES 6-8

1 lb (453 g) dried beans, such as Great Northern

½ tsp white pepper

2 tbsp (30 g) salt

2 tbsp (30 g) dry mustard

1½ tsp (7.5 ml) brown butter

1 cup (201 g) sugar

2 tbsp (30 ml) maple syrup

4 cups (946 ml) water

1 large onion, chopped

1 tbsp (15 ml) vinegar

1 cup (240 g) bacon, cubed, plus more for garnish

Mix the beans, white pepper, salt, mustard, brown butter, sugar, maple syrup and water together in a bowl and allow to soak overnight. Then put the soaked beans and the liquid in a deep pot, add the chopped onion and vinegar, and boil until tender, approximately 40 minutes.

Preheat oven to 250°F (120°C). Lay the cubed bacon across the bottom of a 9 x 9-inch (22.8 x 22.8-cm) casserole dish. When the beans are soft and the husk easily removable, remove beans from the boiling liquid with a wire dipper, and put in the dish with the bacon. Cover the beans with most of the liquid and bake for 3½ hours. Every hour, remove the beans from the oven, stir and add more liquid if needed. Increase oven heat to 400°F (204°C) and bake for another 15 minutes, until top is browned and liquid is bubbling.

Let cool slightly, mix carefully and dish into bean pots. Serve with a slice of fried bacon on top.

[61] For reference information see Endnotes.

HORN & HARDART'S MACARONI AND CHEESE

This tomato-laced dish is about as elegant as macaroni and cheese can get. It's satisfyingly cheesy,
but the tomato adds acid and texture to what often is a one-note dish.

SERVES 4-6

½ lb (226 g) dry elbow macaroni

1¼ tsp (6.25 g) butter

1¼ tsp (6.25 g) flour

½ tsp salt

Dash white pepper

Dash red pepper

1¼ cups (295 ml) milk

2 tsp (10 ml) light cream

1 cup (240 g) cheddar cheese, shredded

½ tsp sugar

½ cup (120 g) canned tomatoes, diced

Cook the macaroni according to directions on the package, then drain and set aside. Preheat the oven to 400°F (204°C). Melt the butter on top of double boiler. Whisk the flour, salt, white and red pepper into the butter gradually. When smooth, add the milk and cream, whisking constantly. Cook for a few minutes until the mixture thickens. Slowly whisk in the cheese and continue to heat until it melts and the sauce looks smooth. Remove from heat. Add the cooked macaroni to the sauce, then add the sugar and tomatoes and stir to combine. Pour mixture into a buttered baking dish and bake until the surface is brown, about 5 to 7 minutes.

Horn & Hardart's Fish Cakes

These fried fish cakes are the perfect Automat dish—a delicate, creamy, fried snack, and likely a way to stretch fish by combining it with potatoes. The fried onions and Worcestershire sauce add depth to what would otherwise be an elaborate fish stick. Be sure to use firm potatoes so the cakes hold their shape. Any flaky, white fish can be substituted for cod.

Makes about 10 cakes

———·———

DIPPING MIXTURE

1 egg

⅔ cup (157 ml) milk

1 tsp (5 g) salt

A dash of white pepper

1 tsp (5 ml) Worcestershire sauce

CAKES

2 tbsp (28 g) butter

2 tbsp (30 g) onions, chopped

1 lb (453 g) firm potatoes, boiled and chopped

½ lb (226 g) cod, boiled

½ tsp white pepper

1 tsp (5 g) parsley, minced

⅔ cup (157 ml) cream

Cracker crumbs

Oil or grease for frying

For the dipping mixture, whisk all the ingredients together in a wide bowl. Set aside.

Heat butter over high heat in a skillet. Add the onions and fry until light brown and crispy, about 5 minutes. Remove with a slotted spoon to a paper towel to let drain. In a food processor, grind together the potatoes and codfish until just combined, but not puréed. In a large bowl, mix together fish mixture, fried onion, white pepper, parsley and cream. Chill for 30 minutes. Once the batter is set, mold into fish cakes weighing 2 ounces (56 g). If the batter is still loose, add cracker crumbs to thicken. Roll the cakes in cracker crumbs until fully coated, then dip them in dipping mixture and then roll them again in the cracker crumbs. Heat about ¼ inch (0.6 cm) of oil or grease in a skillet over high heat, and fry the cakes to a golden brown, about 3 minuets per side. Drain on paper towels. Serve hot.

[62] For reference information see Endnotes.

HORN & HARDART'S CHICKEN SOUP

This is the perfect diner chicken soup, rich and savory, with a golden color and lots of texture thanks to the thickening egg yolks and cornstarch. Eat it on a cold night with lots of crackers.

SERVES 8

¾ cup (142 g) white rice

3 tbsp (45 g) butter

½ lb (226 g) chicken thighs, chopped

2 egg yolks

1 gallon (3.7 L) of chicken stock

3 tbsp (45 g) cornstarch

2 tbsp (30 g) salt

Dash of white pepper

Cook the rice until done, and set aside. Heat the butter in the bottom of a large stockpot over medium heat. Add the chopped chicken meat and cook until almost done, about 8 minutes. Meanwhile, beat the egg yolks into the stock until fully incorporated. When the chicken is done, add the stock mixture and rice to the pot. Dissolve the cornstarch in a little water and add to the stock with the rest of the seasonings. Bring to a boil, and simmer for 10 minutes. Check seasoning and serve hot.

[63] For reference information see Endnotes.

DeRobertis Pasticceria

New York, NY

1904-2014

———·———

I have my own stories about DeRobertis Pasticceria. One is that, for a summer, I worked at a rival pastry shop across the street. It was slightly heartbreaking, as I had always split my business between the two, hoping to keep both alive in the face of my neighborhood's ongoing gentrification. I worried I'd aligned myself against a place I loved. Then one afternoon, a customer came into my pastry shop asking for pignoli, the traditional Italian pine-nut cookie. We were all out, but before she left, the owner stopped her. "Go across the street to DeRobertis" he told her, "they make 'em great over there."

DeRobertis Pasticceria was an old-world pastry shop that managed to survive over 100 years without turning into a parody of itself. It didn't beat you over the head with Italian-American tradition, selling you an overhyped glimpse into the neighborhood's past. What it sold you were really good pastries, baked with care and quality, and served with really good espresso and gave you a wire chair in a tin-ceilinged, tile-floored room in which to enjoy them. It was founded by Paolo DeRobertis, an immigrant from the Bari region of Italy, who originally sold espresso and anisette toast out of a storefront on East 12th Street. In 1904 he rented a bigger space on 1st Avenue between 10th and 11th Streets, and began making more cookies, pastries and ices.

Paolo's son, John, soon took over the business, and in the 1940s he bought the building, securing the pasticceria's future. "If we were subject to someone else's rent increases, we would have never survived," said John DeRobertis Jr.,[64] who eventually took over for his father, and worked to keep the tradition alive while still catering to changing palates, serving sfogliatelle beside croissants, cannoli next to cheese Danish. But no matter the changes, it was always a family business. "When I was a kid, we lived above the store, and my parents were down there working all the time," he told me. "When it'd get busy down there, they'd knock on the steam pipe with a knife, and my brothers and I would fight over who had to go down and help. But still, we helped. We had a sense of pride about the place."

It'd get busy often, especially on Sundays, as the locals made a tradition of stopping by after church, stocking up on pignoli, or during the holidays when orders for their struffoli, a tower of fried dough balls drenched in honey, started to roll in. There's only so much the pasticceria could do to keep up with the times, though, and those traditions started to fall away. "Appetites changed in that neighborhood," said DeRobertis Jr., and while a pasticceria can learn to make new pastries, it can't do much if people don't want pastries at all. "Even though you're busy on the holidays, you have to put that money aside to get you through the slow periods, which were getting longer." However, gentrification wasn't the only factor. Even though they owned the building, summer blackouts and hurricanes became more common in the later years, with insurance companies paying just a fraction of the cost of all the supplies they'd lose. After over 100 years, even the protection of owning the building couldn't save DeRobertis, and it closed in December 2014.

I went to DeRobertis on its last night and by the time I got there it was nearly cleaned out, with just a few cookies and napoleons still on the baking sheets. The old-timers were sharing sentimental hugs, and the woman next to me had seemingly brought in her son for the first time, explaining how often she used to come in the 1970s. "We never realized how much people loved the place until we announced we were closing," said DeRobertis Jr. "People who came in only a few times, started crying. If we were the kind of place worth crying over, we did it naturally. We were surprised, but it made us happy."

DeRobertis Struffoli

Struffoli is an Italian dessert traditionally served during Christmas, a towering pyramid of fried dough drenched with honey and topped with sprinkles or Jordan almonds. This seasonal specialty was mastered by the bakers at DeRobertis, with light, fluffy dough balls and warmed honey that coats every bite.

SERVES 6-10

4 cups (512 g) flour

6 eggs

1 tsp (5 ml) vanilla

½ cup (100 g) sugar

Pinch of salt

½ cup (118 ml) vegetable oil

1 qt (946 ml) honey

Sprinkles or Jordan almonds for garnish (optional)

In a food processor or by hand, mix together flour, eggs, vanilla, sugar and salt. Form the dough into a ball, wrap with cling wrap and chill in the refrigerator for 30 minutes.

Remove the dough from the refrigerator and cut into eight equal sections. Roll each section into a rope, ½ inch (1.25 cm) thick, and cut into ½-inch (1.25-cm) pieces. Roll each piece into a ball and set aside.

In a deep skillet, heat oil to 375°F (190°C). Drop balls in batches into the skillet (careful not to crowd), and fry until they are golden brown, about 2–3 minutes, frequently turning them with a slotted spoon. When done, remove from the skillet to a tray covered with paper towels to let drain.

Heat the honey in a large saucepan until warm and thin, then add the struffoli to the pan. Stir carefully until coated, then remove from heat and continue to stir for another 5 minutes. Turn the struffoli out onto a platter or serving tray, arrange in a pyramid, and either serve as is or decorate with sprinkles or Jordan almonds.

[65] For reference information see Endnotes.

BOB'S CHILI PARLOR

Spokane, WA
1905-1961

In 1979, Jim Sporhase of the *Spokane Chronicle*[66] reminisced in his column about wanting to taste a bowl of Bob's Chili Parlor's namesake dish again. Almost immediately he was flooded with letters from readers all claiming to have the "original" recipe. The paper published six of them, and for weeks after there was a hunt for whether any of them were real. Mrs. Larry Nobles, daughter-in-law of the last owner of the restaurant, claimed one of the recipes that were sent in sounded a lot like the "original," and another man wrote in claiming his wife had the original recipe. Sporhase posted updates in his column "'Round Town," from how "one reader wrote me that she had used parts of three different chili recipes" to concoct something she believed tasted authentic to more thoughts from Mrs. Nobles. Bob's Chili Parlor clearly had made its mark.

Spokane, Washington, is not the place one would think to find chili and tamales at the turn of the century, but in 1905 Robert Cleary opened R. E. Cleary's chili shop, the oldest chili parlor west of the Rockies.[67] It became Bob's Chili Parlor in the 1920s after he lured a local tamale chef into his kitchen. "It's not terribly expected," said Richard Engeman, Pacific Northwest food historian. "There wasn't much of a Mexican or Californian population." However, Engeman notes that wealthier Washingtonians and Oregonians were shopping in San Francisco and spending winters in Pasadena as far back as the 1890s, where it's likely they would have developed more of a taste for Cal-Mex food, and brought it with them when they returned.

Bob's Chili Parlor had an easy time gaining a following, as it was the only Mexican restaurant in town. "It had an instant exoticism," said Engeman. But soon, Bob's became just as famous for giving chili away, and providing the Pacific Northwest with the means to make their own Mexican food. Beginning in 1915 Bob's would host a Christmas Day feast, sometimes serving up to 1,000 people for free. That same year, an ad was placed in the newspaper: "To the Housewife By Bob's Chili Parlor…We will deliver to your home Bob's famous chili recipe, including six other Spanish dishes, with all the necessary prepared Mexican seasonings to make two gallons of chili upon the receipt of $1."[69]

Despite the restaurant's popularity, Cleary seemed to have other creative passions he wanted to pursue. In 1921 he wrote a song called "Bob's Chili Rag," and he filed a copyright for a fox-trot in 1940.[71] He sold his share of the parlor to Harry Nobles in 1927, and Nobles bought out another owner in 1940. In the late 1940s, Duncan Hines listed it in his famous guide, one of only three restaurants in Spokane. It never seemed to lose its popularity, and according to the *Chronicle*, it is only due to the "high rate of production" that Bob's closed in 1961.

If you look at the recipes published in 1979, the one that Mrs. Nobles claimed to be "real" certainly stands out—if only because it yields 30 gallons of chili. The rest are variations on a theme. It's one thing to make people come to you for a new culinary experience, but another to help them create it for themselves. Every one of those recipes is "authentic" to Bob's, because they were inspired by the flavors it provided.

BOB'S CHILI

This chili may as well be called "beef three ways," with chunks of meat, beef tallow and beef stock simmering into a glistening bowl of lightly spiced stew, that was served with plenty of crackers and beer at Bob's counter. Few people have the ability to cook (or eat) 120 pounds (55 kg) of meat, so we've adapted it into an easier to manage portion. Still, you may want to make this when you know you have a lot of mouths to feed.

SERVES 10

7 green bell peppers, chopped

1 oz (28 g) mixed fresh herbs (oregano, parsley, thyme)

Juice of 1 lemon

Salt to taste

A few drops of clove oil

6 lb (2.7 kg) beef, cut into small pieces or coarsely ground

4 cloves garlic, chopped

1 small onion, chopped

Salt to taste

6 bay leaves tied in cheesecloth

2 cups (473 ml) beef tallow, melted

½ tsp cumin

1 tsp (5 g) oregano

2 cups (473 ml) beef stock

½ cup (118 ml) ketchup

To prepare the peppers, take six of the chopped peppers and soak them in warm water for 20 minutes. Pour off the water and blend until fine, then simmer with 3 cups (709 ml) water for about 30 minutes, until it achieves almost the consistency of ketchup. Set aside.

Prepare herb sauce by taking the mixed herbs and simmering them, in 2 cups (473 ml) of water, covered, for 30 minutes. Strain, and add to the water the lemon juice and a pinch of salt, and simmer for 10 minutes. Remove from heat and add the clove oil. Set aside.

Place the meat, garlic, onion, salt, bay leaves and melted tallow in a large pot, and braise over medium heat for about 35 minutes, until red color has come out of the meat. Add cumin, oregano and 1 cup (236 ml) water, and braise for another 15 minutes, then remove the bay leaves, add the pepper sauce and reduce the heat to low. Simmer for half an hour. Stir in the beef stock, the remaining chopped pepper, ketchup and herb sauce, and simmer for another hour.

Bring heat up to high and rapidly boil for 5 minutes, then let rest for half an hour. Skim the fat from the top, check for salt and serve.

[72] For reference information see Endnotes.

Moskowitz & Lupowitz

New York, NY

1909-1966

———·———

We may still have the Jewish deli, but the Jewish Romanian Steakhouse is a style of restaurant that is nearly extinct. Moskowitz & Lupowitz in Manhattan was a shining example of its kind. It was founded in 1909 on Rivington Street by Joseph Moskowitz,[73] a Romanian immigrant who was known for playing jazz around the Lower East Side, and Sam Lupowitz. Soon the restaurant moved to bigger digs on 2nd Street and 2nd Avenue, and Joseph Moskowitz left to pursue a career as a cymbalom player. In 1936 ownership went to Louis Anzelowitz, who kept the original name but also put his own on top of every menu. It was a "carpet joint" with live "gypsy" music, white tablecloths and beef and kasha for $1. It was the type of place where stars like the Marx Brothers and Artie Shaw would hang out. The type of place where Sid Caesar would get married. It was the type of place where stories like this happened.

"One night Bing Crosby and his agent came in for dinner," begins Gary Craig, grandson of owner Louis Anzelowitz.[74] "My grandfather approached the table and asked Bing if he would give the patrons in the dining room a treat and sing a little song. Bing's agent was horrified, but then Bing mentioned to Louis that if he had this very rare scotch (apparently so rare that nobody had any of it) he would agree to sing. My grandfather said, 'What year?' Bing said, 'What do you mean, what year? There isn't a drop of it anywhere.' Again Louis said, 'Give me a year.' Bing said, '1939.' What he didn't know is that my grandfather had, locked upstairs, every year that scotch was made. He came back to the table with three shot glasses and the bottle. Bing's chin hit the table. The next thing you know, my grandfather stood in the middle of the dining room and said, 'Ladies and Gentlemen, I'd like to present Mr. Bing Crosby who's going to sing "Melancholy Baby" for you right now.'"

New York City's Jewish cuisine has now been reduced to the territory of the deli and the bubbie, both delicious and romantic in their own rights, but distinctly lower class. However, in the heyday of the city's Jewish immigration, the Romanian steakhouse became a more sophisticated culinary center. Places like Moskowitz & Lupowitz symbolized the good life so many had immigrated to achieve. It made Jewish life and culture desirable and aspirational. If you hit it big, maybe you could be like the big shots, noshing on chopped liver at M&L while Bing Crosby popped in to sing.

It also provided the kinds of cuisines immigrants associated with the opulence of America. In the "old country," beef was a rare luxury, but in America it was plentiful and cheap, and shaped the future of Jewish-American cuisine. Cuts like Delmonico steak and filet mignon were featured heavily on the menu,[75] as well as more elaborate Romanian main courses like stuffed cabbage, broiled lamb tongue and Romanian sausages. But the

appetizers were where it was proven that this was no "traditional" steakhouse. Diners could order stuffed derma, "icra de schtuka"—a Romanian pike caviar dish, and a variety of herring. According to Craig, "the jewel of the menu" was the chopped liver. "Celebrities would come downtown from the Upper East and West Sides just to have it, and nobody in the city made it the way Moskowitz & Lupowitz did." Most recipes for chopped liver call for chicken liver, a cheap protein plentifully found. But Moskowitz & Lupowitz's recipe uses beef liver. This is America, after all.

The restaurant closed in 1966, the building bought by La Salle Academy to serve as annex classroom and office space. There are few Romanian steakhouses left in New York, the cuisine having split between the filets of the fancier, less Jewish restaurants and the herring and liver of the delis. Moskowitz & Lupowitz was of a time when you didn't have to choose.

MOSKOWITZ & LUPOWITZ'S CHOPPED LIVER

Gary Craig says Jewish celebrities would come all the way "from uptown" for the restaurant's chopped liver, which is made with beef liver rather than the traditional chicken liver. This gives it a richness most recipes lack, while the eggs keep it mousse-like in texture.

SERVES 6-8

2 tbsp (30 ml) olive oil

2 onions, sliced

½ lb (225 g) beef liver

Salt and pepper to taste

4 hard-boiled eggs

Crackers or toasted rye bread, to serve

Heat the olive oil in a skillet over medium heat. Add the onions and cook for 5 minutes, until they begin to soften. Push the onions to the side and add the liver, salt and pepper to the pan, cooking until the liver is browned on both sides, approximately another 5 minutes. Add the liver and onion mixture and the eggs to a food processor, and pulse until it's almost smooth, but still retains texture.

Chill in the refrigerator for at least 4 hours for flavors to blend. Serve on crackers or toasted rye bread.

ASHKENAZ'S DELI

Chicago, IL
1910-2012

———

The Jewish delicatessen is a distinctly American invention. While the deli as marketplace—where a family bought their cold cuts and fish, pickles and relishes—came from the old country, the deli as restaurant was an invention of the new. As the supermarket became the one-stop for food shopping, delis embraced a new identity as dining establishment, where Jews (and eventually others) could enjoy corned beef sandwiches and pickled herring outside the home, and where they could find community at a time when they were often unwelcome in other establishments. Ashkenaz's Deli in Chicago, home to the town's "Blintz King," was one such hub.

The timeline is murky, but it goes something like this: George and Ada (or Ida) Ashkenaz immigrated to Chicago from Russia in the early 1900s, early comers in a wave of immigration that would reshape Chicago's population. They opened a small deli downtown in 1910, but by then the city's Jews were increasingly moving north and west to the suburbs, so they followed and opened Ashkenaz's in Rogers Park. It found a large client base—by 1927, Chicago had the third-largest Jewish population in the world,[76] and the 1908 extension of the "L" turned Rogers Park into an accessible neighborhood for many of them. Ashkenaz's "was sort of Jew central for Rogers Park," according to Jason Diamond, whose family frequented Ashkenaz's.[77] This was especially true after WW II, as even more Jews moved from the South Side to the wealthier suburbs.

George and Ada's son, Sam, took over operations in 1940 after the building burned down, and earned his reputation as Chicago's "Blintz King." But they served everything you'd expect to find in a classic deli—corned beef, smoked fish, chopped liver, bagels and cheesecake that many defended as the best in the country. By all accounts, lines were regularly out the door. "The tone is of a family gathering," read a *Chicago Tribune* article from 1970,[78] and it was a family where everyone was equal. "Saul Bellow would go there whenever he was in that part of town, Dick Butkus of the Chicago Bears ate there, and they all got the same treatment from the servers," said Diamond. There may have been plenty of delis for Chicagoans to choose from, but Ashkenaz's was where they went to hang out.

By 1976, times were changing, and Sam Ashkenaz tried to change with them. He moved the deli to a location further out in the suburbs, where more of the city's Jewish population was relocating now that they had the financial security to do so. "I don't think there'll be so much kibitzing anymore," Sam told a reporter.[79] "I have to go with the times, and it seems like the younger generation just doesn't appreciate this kind of food." Though there seemed to be no shortage of people around to lament its departure. One article claimed Rogers Park would "never be the same" after the move. "Ashkenazi Delicatessen was a fixture. A pole star. Something always there, like Wrigley Field, Lake Michigan or Richard J. Daley."[80]

Though the ownership was the same, the character was gone. Higher meat prices meant the requests for a "taste" while waiting for your order to come up had to be ignored, and while the new location was plush, plush is not what one wants from a deli. One wants years of pickle juice and pastrami grease seeped into the walls, the smell of curing wafting onto the street, and people who treat the owners like family and the restaurant like their living room. Ashkenaz retired, the business moved, the old building burned down and a corporation took over. The deli that still bore his name closed in 2012, after years of business decline.

New York is a city that wears its Jewish culinary history on its sleeve, but when Chicago's Jews moved to the suburbs, they often took those cultural markers with them. Chicago cuisine is more heavily associated with its Irish, Italian and Polish populations. But that doesn't mean Chicago can't claim its Jewish heritage. After all, Polish Jews were partially responsible for the city's ubiquitous Vienna hot dog. In 1989, relative Steve Ashkenaz became the manager of Cirlasky's deli in Chicago, and the paper raved that the city would finally have a "New York–style deli."[81] But the Jewish deli is an institution with deep roots in cities like Chicago. Ashkenaz's embodied everything great about deli culture, New York or not.

ASHKENAZ'S BLINTZ TREAT

This recipe is what earned Sam Ashkenaz the nickname the "Blintz King." The delicate batter provides the lightest crêpes that surround a sweet and savory filling, lightly fried to give a slight crisp.

MAKES 6 BLINTZES

CRÊPES

1 cup (128 g) all-purpose flour

1¼ cups (295 ml) water

Pinch salt

Vegetable oil (for cooking)

CHEESE MIX

1 lbs (453 g) dried farmers cheese or dried baker's cheese

1 egg

6 tbsp (90 g) sugar

Sour cream, apple sauce and sugared blueberries to garnish

To make the crêpes, heat an 8-inch (20-cm) pan over medium-low heat. Whisk together the flour, water and salt, and grease the pan lightly with vegetable oil or butter, using a towel to apply so all corners of the pan are covered. When the pan is hot, pour about half a ladle of batter into the pan, and turn the pan to spread it as thin as possible. When the crêpe begins to curl (after about a minute), flip it onto a paper towel.

For the filling, stir together the cheese and eggs, sprinkling sugar on top of the mixture as you turn it in. The mixture should still be firm. Lay about ¼ cup (60 ml) of the mixture on the blintz in a 4-inch (10-cm) row. Fold the sides of the crêpe over, and roll the blintz back to front. Heat a half-inch (1.25 cm) of vegetable oil in a pan. Once the oil is hot, fry blintzes (being sure not to crowd the pan) for 2–3 minutes per side, until they're lightly golden and crispy. Remove blintzes to a paper towel to drain, and place on a heated serving platter.

Serve with sour cream or apple sauce, and sugared blueberries.

[82] For reference information see Endnotes.

Ye Olde College Inn

Houston, TX
1919-1980s

———·——

College eateries are rarely held up as examples of fine, or even mildly enjoyable, cuisine. A plate of mozzarella sticks at 3 a.m. is surely satisfying, but nothing to write home about or even mention. According to its history, Ye Old College Inn wasn't that kind of place. It became a city landmark, welcoming Rice University students, alumni and the larger community, especially if they were football fans. They also may have invented loaded baked potatoes.

Ye Old College Inn started as The Owl in 1919, across the street from Rice University, which had only been around for a few years. "From it's beginning, it was intimately tied to the life of the campus, and in particular the life of athletics," according to Melissa Kean of Rice University.[83] At the time, Rice University was beyond the edge of the city, and there was not much for students, or administrators, to do around campus. George Martin bought the Owl (which had been named for the school's mascot), and by 1921, he had expanded it and given it a new name. At the beginning, it still had more in common with your average college eatery, a place where "boys would always shoot craps…until George in desperation would turn out the lights to try to make them leave."[84] However, by the 1950s it would be known as "Houston's oldest fine restaurant."

Ye Old College Inn became a gathering point, and headquarters for everyone from faculty to athletes to visiting celebrities. And Martin, as a football fan, made it the home for all things Rice football, even presenting his own MVP trophy. The George Martin award is a "top honor that is bestowed annually on a Rice football player" given by "veteran Owl fan George Martin, who has seen every Rice team in history play virtually every game," according to a clip from Martin's scrapbook.[85] This was easy, considering the restaurant was located across the street from Rice's stadium, and it soon became customary to celebrate games at Ye Old College Inn, largely because there were no other options. "By the time there were other things, it was just such an ingrained tradition," says Kean.

While Ye Old College Inn was one of Houston's few finer-dining options, it was still in Texas. A fine meal meant steak and potatoes, washed down with some whiskey, catering to the "big rich" of Texas's oil boom. Ye Old College Inn aimed to please. They made a name for themselves by being the first place in Houston (and possibly the U.S.) to offer "rubbed, tubbed and scrubbed" baked potatoes, loaded with cheese, chives, bacon and sour cream.[86] But the restaurant also became known for its Gulf-influenced cuisine, especially rich seafood dishes featuring gulf shrimp and oysters, heavily seasoned to provide the big flavors the football players craved.

In 1945 Ernest Coker took over as the proprietor, and a few years later hired a chef named Herman Walker, who had been cooking since he was a child on the Gulf Coast. "[The Gulf Coast] is well known for its seafood cuisine, and that's what they subsisted on, a lot of shrimp and other seafood," said Craig Manson, Walker's grand-nephew.[87] Walker learned to cook with his sister, and eventually followed her to Houston, where he found a number of jobs cooking at restaurants, and eventually wound up at Ye Old College Inn. By 1967, he had "won awards and prizes over the years, and praise from experts in all parts of the country," including for the "subtly garlicky Shrimp Herman."[88] However, the recipe is identical to one for "Shrimp Ernie" that Coker published in in the late 1940s. Perhaps it was better advertising that the recipes came from the chef rather than the owner, and Walker went on to adapt many other of Coker's recipes, adding his own flavors to them.

Walker worked at Ye Old College Inn for almost fifty years, cooking for athletes, celebrities and anyone else who rented out the Varsity Room for special events. But in the 1980s, the building was razed to make way for a new medical tower. Nowadays many mentions of its history are as a footnote, just one of many viable Houston restaurants, or perhaps the city's top restaurant for a time, but the top restaurant in a city that was more rough and tumble than refined. It was a big fish in a small pond, but the pond got bigger. Ye Old College Inn turned into a relic of a Houston that doesn't exist anymore.

Ye Olde College Inn's Shrimp Ernie

Ketchup may not seem like the sort of ingredient you want on anything other than fries, but broiled down and caramelized with the spices in this recipe it becomes a flavorful sauce for these perfectly cooked shrimp.

Serves 6-8

2 cups (473 ml) vegetable oil

1 tsp (5 g) salt

4 tbsp (60 ml) ketchup

1 tsp (5 g) paprika

1 clove garlic, crushed

2 lb (907 g) shrimp, peeled and deveined

Mix together the oil, salt, ketchup, paprika and garlic, and pour over prepared shrimp. Let marinate for 1 to 2 hours in the refrigerator. Heat a broiler to medium. Remove the shrimp from the marinade and lay them in a single layer in a baking dish, then pour the marinade over the shrimp, enough that the shrimp sits in it but is not covered. Broil for 3 minutes, then flip and broil for another 3 on the other side. Remove the shrimp to a platter and serve with toothpicks.

[230] For reference information see Endnotes.

YE OLDE COLLEGE INN'S HERMAN'S FUDGE PIE

In 1959, Ye Olde College Inn released a small booklet of recipes, celebrating their 40th anniversary. In it is a recipe for "Ernie's Fudge Pie," presumably named for the proprietor at the time, Ernie Coker. In 1967, The Milwaukee Sentinel *published an article about Ye Olde College Inn with a recipe for "Herman's Many Prized Fudge Pie," named for the Inn's longtime chef, Herman Walker. Walker's recipe featured "several small and excellent" changes to the original, fudgy recipe, including the addition of instant coffee, which really enhances the chocolate flavor.*

SERVES 6-8

½ cup (113 g) butter

3 oz (85 g) unsweetened baking chocolate

4 eggs

3 tbsp (44 ml) light corn syrup

1½ cups (300 g) sugar

1 tsp (5 g) instant coffee

1 tsp (5 ml) vanilla

¼ tsp salt

⅛ tsp ground cinnamon

⅛ tsp ground allspice

9-inch (22.8-cm) pastry-lined pie pan

Vanilla ice cream for topping

Preheat the oven to 350°F (176°C). Melt the butter and baking chocolate in the microwave or a double boiler, and set aside. Meanwhile, beat the eggs until light, then add corn syrup, sugar, coffee, vanilla, salt, cinnamon and allspice, and stir until combined. Add the chocolate mixture to the egg mixture and mix thoroughly. Pour into the prepared pie pan, and bake until the top is crusty and the filling is set but soft inside, so that it shakes like a custard when pulled out, about 25 minutes. Serve with a small scoop of vanilla ice cream on top.

Ye Olde College Inn's Oysters Ernie

Oysters Ernie was one of the most well-known recipes from Ye Olde College Inn, an appetizer of lightly fried oysters served with a thick, tart dipping sauce that brings out the meatiness of the oysters.

Serves 4

Salt and pepper

24 oysters

2 tbsp (16 g) flour, plus more
for dredging

4 tbsp (60 g) butter

¼ cup (60 lm) lemon juice

1 cup (236 ml) A1 steak sauce

2 tbsp (30 ml) Worcestershire sauce

3 oz (88 ml) madeira wine

3 tbsp (44 ml) water

Salt and pepper the oysters, then dredge them in flour. Melt 1½ tablespoons (22 g) butter on a griddle, and pan-fry the oysters until crisp and browned, about 5 minutes. Melt ½ tablespoon (8 g) butter, and sprinkle it over the oysters while cooking. Meanwhile, mix the remaining 2 tablespoons (30 g) butter, lemon juice, steak sauce, Worcestershire and madeira in a saucepan over low heat. Blend 2 tablespoons (16 g) flour into water and whisk it into sauce once heated to thicken. Place oysters in a serving plate and dress with the heated sauce.

MT. NITTANY INN

Centre Hall, PA
1919-2014

———·——

In 1989, Sue Hubbell embarked on a cross-country taste test of America's pies for her book, what the *New Yorker*[89] called in an excerpt, "The Great American Pie Expedition." She zigzagged across the country, collecting recipes and tips, tasting Shaker lemon pies and banana cream pies and opining on what makes great crusts and fillings. One pie she never tasted, though, to her lament, was the peanut butter pie at Mt. Nittany Inn just outside of Centre Hall, Pennsylvania, smack in the middle of the state. The multiple times she went, it was out of stock for some reason, but the proprietor told her the pie, made by his wife, was worth the hype. "She makes the peanut butter all creamy, and then she freezes it," he said. "But I don't know what all she puts into it. A lot of stuff. Cheese, maybe?"

Cream cheese, to be specific, along with whipped cream and powdered sugar and a lot of peanut butter. It's the kind of pie that transforms its ingredients, a recipe that you'd spend your life holding in reverence, and then when you finally got your hands on it, would think "That's it?" That sort of satisfying simplicity, as well as the Inn's astounding view, is what drew customers for almost a hundred years.

Mt. Nittany Inn began in 1919 as a roadside stand called Pete's Place, opened by Pete Coldren, a rest stop for people crossing the mountain. It had no competition, but still began surprising visitors to the remote region with its food. "Back on Center Hall mountain, too, I encountered an innovation," wrote one traveler.[90] "The woman at Pete Coldren's eating place actually buttered two hamburg sandwiches for me and my girl-friend . . . butter on a sandwich at a roadside eating place is as scarce as an Al Smith vote at W.T.C.U. Headquarters," a joke about the bubbling prohibition movement in the United States. The anonymous author noted Coldren had a "nice place . . . quite a change in that mountain."

In 1933, Coldren obtained a liquor license (the oldest in the state according to some reports) and expanded the restaurant into Mount Nittany Coffee Shop. The food was straightforward—hamburg sandwiches, steaks, chops—but the view from the mountain is what turned it into a spot. Couples would eat burgers and listen to the jukebox, or look at the view of Penn's Valley. By the 1960s Coldren had sold it, and it was being run mainly as a bar. At some point it closed, because in 1975 when Bill Zang bought it, it was completely run down and boarded up. "I would hear my father talk about Central Pennsylvania," said Jeanne Zang, Bill's daughter.[91] "He always wanted to go back. In 1975, people said he was crazy when he quit his job of almost 20 years to buy this rundown place on top of Mt. Nittany." Bill's son Jon also remembers "pulling up in front of that place on that cold, foggy April morning. I could not believe the ungodly shape that this place was in." The Zang family fixed it up and reopened it as the Mt. Nittany Inn, with a bed and breakfast and some of Bill's wife, Betty's desserts.

The Inn continued as an iconic space in the area, for everything from date-night dinners to wedding receptions, the view cementing its customer base even as it changed ownership. It was even enough to help the Inn come back after it burned down not once, but twice, in 2003 and 2004, but those fires marked the beginning of the end. Nancy Silvis, the last owner, said the business[92] took a hit, and rising food costs made things even harder for independently owned businesses. The recession of 2008 made it even worse, and they never quite recovered. By 2014 it was time to close.

Places like the Mt. Nittany Inn often become accidental landmarks. There's nothing particularly remarkable about them—no innovative cuisine, no historic firsts. They are not where the celebrities go, but they are where the community goes. And when they're gone, they are missed as much as anything.

Mt. Nittany Inn's Peanut Butter Pie

Most peanut butter pies are thick, heavy concoctions that stick to the top of your mouth, but this airy, frozen pie is rich in peanut butter flavor without the need for a cold glass of milk. It's perfect for any party, especially in the summer, since you don't even have to turn the oven on to make it.

Makes 2 pies

1¼ cups (283 g) cream cheese

¾ cup (135 g) peanut butter

1¼ cups (295 ml) cold milk

2½ cups (312 g) confectioners sugar

2½ cups (590 ml) heavy whipping cream

1¼ tsp (6 ml) vanilla

2 graham cracker crusts

Whisk the cream cheese and peanut butter together until fully incorporated. Add the milk and sugar and mix until smooth. Separately, whip the heavy cream and vanilla together until stiff peaks form. Fold together the whipped cream and cream cheese mixtures, and divide evenly between the crusts. Freeze for several hours until firm.

[93] For reference information see Endnotes.

Mt. Nittany Inn's Clam Chowder

Mt. Nittany Inn's clam chowder recipe came from the Zang family's personal collection, a simple, straightforward chowder that was always a hit on the menu. Lightly browning the bacon helps it keep shape and crunch in the rich stew, giving it a variety of textures.

SERVES 6-8

¼ lb (113 g) bacon, chopped

1 cup (240 g) chopped onion

2 lb (907 g) potatoes, peeled and diced

1¼ lb (566 g) chopped clams

¼ cup (60 g) clam base

¼ tsp thyme

¼ tsp salt

¼ tsp white pepper

5½ cups (1.3 L) water

¼ lb (113 g) butter

¾ cup (96 g) flour

4 cups (946 ml) milk

Sauté the bacon and onion together in a skillet over medium heat, until onion is translucent and the bacon just begins to brown, about 10 minutes. Separately, boil the potatoes until tender. In a large stock pot, combine the bacon, onions, potatoes and clams, straining some of the juice first. Add the clam base, thyme, salt and white pepper, and cover with water. Bring to a boil, then cover and let simmer for 30 minutes.

Meanwhile, in a small saucepan over medium heat, whisk the butter and flour together to form a light roux, about 10 minutes. Add milk and bring to a boil, then let simmer for 25 minutes. Add milk mixture to the soup, mix and simmer together for another 5 minutes.

[94] For reference information see Endnotes.

THE NEW YORK EXCHANGE
FOR WOMEN'S WORK

New York, NY

1919-1980

In 1878, the repercussions of the Civil War were still being felt, especially for women who lost husbands or fathers. Many women were uneducated and untrained for any sort of work, and thus discovered they were unable to support themselves or their families. To help these women achieve financial independence, Mrs. William G. Choate, Candace Wheeler and approximately 20 other women founded the New York Exchange for Women's Work.

The Exchange began as a way to "assist ladies who desired to replenish their slender purses without making it known to the world," according to *The Art Amateur*,[95] though it certainly embodied early ideals of feminism, giving women a resourceful way to support their families after they were widowed, abandoned or their husbands just lost the family fortune. The skills these women often did possess were of the domestic arts, and through the Exchange they filled orders for clothing, paintings and homemade jams. Eventually, the Exchange opened a Vocational Bureau in order to help some of these women find work. However, needlepoint can't always pay the rent, which is why the Exchange opened a restaurant.

The Exchange Restaurant opened in 1919, as the Exchange moved its headquarters to twin buildings at 539-541 Madison Avenue. It "became a place to eat well and inexpensively and to be seen," according to the *New York Times*,[96] selling "bittersweet chocolate cake and home-baked crab cakes, codfish balls and wedding cakes." It was a place for tea and snacks, or sometimes a larger meal, all based on recipes provided by the women it employed, and with proceeds returning to them. In 1934, post-Prohibition, the Exchange opened the Crinoline Bar next door.

Part of the appeal was the ability for women to eat and drink in public without male accompaniment. In 1971, just after famed downtown bar McSorley's began to allow women in, writer Betty Rollin told *New York* magazine[97] that the Exchange restaurant "makes you feel you've stepped out of New York and into an old ladies' home…These women can feel confident here. Nothing nasty can ever happen at the Women's Exchange."

The restaurant's menu history,[98] which spans from 1934 through 1980, also showcases New York's changing tastes. The earliest menus feature chicken aspic with mayonnaise for 60 cents, and roast oysters with coleslaw for 75. By the 1960s "whipped codfish balls" made an appearance, and the last menu offered Chicken a la King for $4. Recipes from the women were also available in the Exchange's newsletters, and homemade goods were often sold in the store alongside the crafts.

Unfortunately, popularity has its drawbacks. In the 1970s, the IRS began to question the restaurant's tax-exempt status, concluding that the restaurant itself did not serve the Exchange's charitable mission and would need to become a for-profit establishment. The restaurant closed permanently in 1980, and the rest of the Exchange closed in 2003 amid rising rents.

A woman's home cooking, though often beloved, is rarely put front and center in a restaurant setting. Instead it is usually paid homage to by others, and usually by men. The New York Exchange for Women's Work didn't feature mom's Sunday meals reimagined and elevated by a professional chef, but the dishes themselves, made by women and for women, and for the benefit of women. It wasn't inspired by the thing, it was the thing itself.

EXCHANGE RESTAURANT'S CHEDDAR HA PENNIES

These snacks are essentially small, savory cheese cookies. The recipe was found in a cookbook published by the Exchange, featuring recipes submitted by its members that were often made and sold in the restaurant and store. The recipe calls for these cookies, equally fluffy and crisp, to be served warm "with cocktails."

MAKES ABOUT 20 COOKIES

½ cup (113 g) butter, softened

1 cup (128 g) sifted flour

½ lb (225 g) sharp cheddar cheese, grated

¼ tsp salt

3 tbsp (45 g) dry onion soup mix

Preheat the oven to 350°F (176°C). Cut the butter and flour together until fully incorporated. Add the cheese, salt and soup mix to the flour and butter and mix until combined. Roll the mixture into balls approximately ¾ inch (2 cm) in diameter, and place on a lightly oiled baking sheet. Bake for approximately 15 minutes, until balls form a light outer crust.

[99] For reference information see Endnotes.

EXCHANGE RESTAURANT'S BLOODY MARY SOUP

This is either a heavily flavored tomato soup or a Bloody Mary in a bowl. Either way, it's genius.
The vodka adds bite without any real alcohol content, and there's the lingering taste of celery without
having to deal with a gigantic stalk sticking out of your glass.

SERVES 6

2 tbsp (30 g) butter

1 onion, diced

3 celery stalks, diced

2 tbsp (30 ml) tomato purée

1 tbsp (15 g) sugar

5 cups (1.2 L) tomato juice

1 tbsp (15 g) salt

1 tbsp (15 ml) lemon juice

Black pepper to taste

Worcestershire sauce to taste

4 oz (30 ml) vodka

In a large saucepan, melt the butter over medium heat. Sauté the onion and celery in butter until the onion begins to caramelize, about 15 minutes. Add the tomato puree and sugar and stir together for a minute, then add the tomato juice and bring to a simmer. Let simmer for 8 minutes, and add the remaining ingredients. Strain, then return to the saucepan and bring to a boil. Serve hot with another dash of Worcestershire sauce on top.

[100] For reference information see Endnotes.

Exchange Restaurant's Cold Curry Soup

This would have been an elegant dish to eat alongside your fellow women at the New York Exchange for Women's Work. The apples and celery bring a freshness and crisp texture to the chilled soup. For the best flavor, make your own curry powder blend instead of using one that's been sitting on the grocery store shelves for months.

SERVES 6

2 tbsp (30 g) butter

3 onions, chopped

1 tart apple, chopped

3 stalks celery, chopped

1 green bell pepper, chopped

1 garlic clove

Salt to taste

1 pinch cayenne pepper

1 tbsp (15 g) curry powder

6 cups (1.4 L) chicken stock

½ cup (120 g) white rice

2 tbsp (30 ml) lemon juice

Watercress leaves for garnish

Heat the butter in a large Dutch oven or pot over medium heat. Add the onions and cook until soft but not browned, about 10 minutes. Add the apple, celery, pepper and garlic and cook until they're softened, about 5 minutes. Season with salt, cayenne and curry powder, stirring to combine, then add the chicken stock. Bring the soup to a boil, then cover and lower heat to simmer for about 30 minutes. Add the rice, and cook another 20 minutes. Let cool, then purée in a blender with the lemon juice.

Chill, and serve cold with watercress leaves on each.

[101] For reference information see Endnotes.

THE MARAMOR

Columbus, OH

1920-1970s

On the occasion of its 35th year in 1955, a promotional ad for the Maramor in Columbus, Ohio, outlined the principles that led to its success: to provide a happy place for people to work, to please the customer and to pay the bills. It was a simple mission, but one that led the Maramor to be one of the most celebrated restaurants in the area at the time.

The Maramor was founded in 1920 by Mary Love. According to the census from that year she was living on East Broad Street, where the Maramor would first open, and the manager of the tea room at the F&R Lazarus Department Store. She soon established the Maramor tea room in the Benjamin Brown home at 112 East Broad Street,[102] named as a contraction of her name, were it in Spanish (Maria Amor). In 1929, the *Ohio Jewish Chronicle* wrote that the Maramor "was not only a restaurant, but a natural market" for baked goods and candies, for which they soon became known. "The Maramor Restaurant, and the Maramor candies, now have a reputation from the Atlantic to the Pacific, and the Maramor is known as one of the unique shops of its kind in the United States."[103] An author at the *Hotel Monthly* also named it "without a doubt the most attractive tea room he found."[104]

The Maramor was perfectly timed to become as popular as it did. The 1920s and '30s were a booming time for the restaurant industry, as urban populations grew and more people found themselves living in smaller accommodations with smaller, or nonexistent, kitchens. This made dining out more of a necessity. At the same time, women were increasingly looking for work outside the home, and kitchen work was a logical extension of the home care duties many women had already been tasked with. The staff of the Maramor was overwhelmingly female. Love and husband Malcolm McGuckin made a point of employing college-trained women,[105] and ensuring they had a comfortable and supportive place to work. The restaurant even did away with tips, presumably by raising costs to ensure the employees were paid a fair wage. Love also oversaw the specifics of how things were cooked, which varied from typical restaurant kitchens. "Instead of cooking in tremendous kettles, all food is cooked in small quantities as the meal progresses," according to a promotional booklet released in the 1930s,[106] which also noted that all the chocolates made at their adjoining gift shop contained no preservatives or artificial ingredients. Today they would have just gone with "artisanal."

The restaurant quickly became one of the most popular in downtown Columbus. It was known for its simple, delicate, but fashionable food, like Chicken a la King and eggs benedict. More than anything, though, they were known for their desserts, all made from scratch and often from the recipes of home cooks. Things like fresh coconut cake with homemade coconut cream, chocolate almond mint meringue and their famous "floating island"—a custard-like dessert topped with meringue—were known to all who dined there. The Maramor eventually attracted the palate of food reviewer Duncan Hines. In his column "Adventures in Good Eating," he regularly praised the restaurant's "light as a feather" chicken dumplings, vegetable soup that was "truly a meal in itself," and when he recommended that customers tour the workings of the kitchen, the Maramor had to start booking kitchen tours two months in advance. "I'm always delighted when my journey takes me through Columbus, Ohio, for then I'll have at least one meal at The Maramor Restaurant," he wrote in his 1955 autobiography.

The Maramor grew to not just a restaurant, but a cocktail lounge called Maramor Lane, and they were as known for their chocolates and gift shop as they were for the restaurant itself. But in the 1950s the business began to change. In 1945 the McGuckins had sold it to Maurice Sher, who later brought on Danny Deeds as a manager. The two agreed that patronage was slipping due to the popular notion that the Maramor was only a "tea room" that catered to the tastes of women, and set out to attract a younger crowd and more men. "People seem to need a reason for eating out," Deeds told a local paper. "We are going to give them one." With that, he began to bring in national acts like Duke Ellington, Phyllis Diller and the Smothers Brothers, making the Maramor the nightclub of Columbus. But the Maramor followed a similar path of many restaurants in the 1960s. Suburban sprawl and decentralization took people away from downtown, and in 1969 the restaurant closed, focusing on its chocolate business. A tea room may sound like an antiquated establishment, but a restaurant that served fresh food, treated its workers fairly and was run by women? How very modern.

MARAMOR'S HOT TODDY

In a handwritten collection of notes and recipes of the Maramor is this simple hot toddy recipe, with just a touch of warming spices. It's meant to be enjoyed with a quick dessert or a few chocolates in the Maramor's tea room.

SERVES 1

1½ oz (44 ml) bourbon

2 tsp (10 ml) honey

2 dashes Angostura bitters

⅔ scant tsp ground allspice

2 cloves

Lemon zest spiral for garnish

Nutmeg for garnish

Combine all ingredients (except garnishes) in an 8-ounce (236-ml) mug, and fill with boiling water. Let steep for a minute, then garnish with a lemon zest spiral and freshly grated nutmeg.

[107] For reference information see Endnotes.

Maramor's Vegetable Soup

This recipe was printed by Duncan Hines, a noted fan of the "charming Maramor," in his "Adventures in Good Eating" column through the Bell Syndicate wire service in 1949.[108] The soup relies on salt as its only seasoning, letting the market's worth of vegetables shine on their own (though there is some beef stock to pump it up). Definitely try using fresh vegetables all the way through if you can get them.

SERVES 8

½ cup (120 g) carrots, diced

½ cup (120 g) green pepper, diced

½ cup (120 g) celery, diced

¼ cup (60 g) onion, diced

½ cup (120 g) cabbage, chopped

½ cup (120 g) potatoes, diced

1 tbsp (15 g) salt

⅓ cup (80 g) fresh or canned okra

⅓ cup (80 g) fresh or canned corn

2 cups (480 g) canned tomatoes

1 qt (946 ml) beef stock

Salt to taste

Combine the carrots, pepper, celery, onion, cabbage, potatoes and salt in a deep stock pot. Just cover with water and boil for 15 minutes, being sure they don't get mushy. Add the okra, corn, tomatoes and stock and bring to a boil. Let boil for another 5 minutes, then remove from heat and let stand for one hour. Salt the soup to taste, reheat and serve.

MARAMOR'S CHRISTMAS PECAN COOKIES

This recipe comes from some handwritten records from the Maramor, now kept at the Columbus Historical Society.
They come out slightly crisp on the outside and fluffy on the inside, with lots of rich caramel and brown sugar flavors.
Add the flour a little at a time, stopping when the dough just begins to come together.

MAKES ABOUT 30 COOKIES

⅝ cup (141 g) butter

1¼ cups (255 g) brown sugar

⅝ cup (148 ml) light corn syrup

1 egg

½ cup (118 ml) caramel syrup

2 tbsp (30 ml) whole milk

4 cups (400 g) pastry flour

1 tsp (5 g) baking powder

¼ tsp cinnamon

¼ tsp salt

½ tsp vanilla extract

3½ oz (100 g) sliced pecans

Preheat the oven to 375°F (190°C).

Cream together the butter, sugar and corn syrup. Beat in the egg until fully combined, then add the caramel syrup and milk. In a separate bowl, sift together the flour, baking powder, cinnamon and salt, and beat into the creamed mixture by thirds until fully combined. Lastly, add the vanilla and sliced pecans until combined. Cover and chill the dough for half an hour.

Flour a flat surface and roll the dough out to ¼-inch (6-mm) thick. Cut cookies with a round cookie cutter about 2 inches (5 cm) in diameter. Transfer them to a greased cookie sheet and bake for approximately 10 minutes, until browned around the edges. Let cool on a rack before serving.

Maramor's Floating Island

This recipe for one of the Maramor's most beloved desserts was printed in the Columbus Dispatch. *The recipe used in the restaurant allegedly originated with Gwendolyn Pavey. Floating Island is reminiscent of an elegant Baked Alaska, a thick custard topped with a soft meringue that is browned, then chilled for a refreshing but rich flavor.*

SERVES 4

3 eggs, separated

¼ cup + 2 tbsp (75 g) sugar

⅛ tsp salt

1 tbsp (15 g) cornstarch

2 cups (473 ml) milk

1½ tsp (7.3 ml) vanilla

Freshly grated nutmeg to taste

Beat the egg yolks and whisk in ¼ cup (50 g) sugar, the salt and cornstarch. Scald the milk in a double boiler over low heat. Slowly add the egg mixture and stir until it thickens, being sure not to let the eggs curdle. Remove from heat and add 1 teaspoon (5 ml) vanilla, and let the custard cool.

Meanwhile, beat the egg whites with the remaining sugar and remaining vanilla until the mixture forms soft peaks. Transfer the cooled custard into an oven-proof serving dish. Top with the meringue and sprinkle lightly with freshly grated nutmeg. Place under a broiler for 2 minutes or until meringue is brown. Chill thoroughly, and serve.

[109] For reference information see Endnotes.

ROGERS' RESTAURANT

Lexington, KY

1923-2004

———•——

When people pine for food, it's always grandma's, sometimes regardless of how grandma actually cooked. Grandma's cooking evokes thoughts of warmth, comfort and safety, nothing too fancy but always exactly what you want. It's something that's incredibly difficult to re-create in a successful restaurant—if it's too innovative, it's not like grandma's, but if it's too simple, well, why pay for what you can get at home? Rogers' Restaurant in Kentucky managed to walk that line well for over 80 years.

Founded in 1923 by George Owens Rogers, it was by many accounts Lexington's oldest continuously operated dining establishment. He opened it in the site of a former confectionary with $100 borrowed from his grandmother, but by the late 1930s it was so popular, there were three branches around the city. Rogers featured home-style cooking, everything from fried chicken to salmon croquettes to hams that Rogers cured himself from the hogs he raised on his farm. In 1964 the restaurant moved locations, and ten years later Charles Ellinger bought the restaurant from Rogers as a Valentine's Day gift for his wife, Jan. Their family owned it for the next three generations.

Rogers may also have a bit of a checkered past—Jan Ellinger says they discovered a wall full of telephone lines when they bought the place, suggesting it had been a bookie joint. "A bartender, 'Shorty' Walker, told me $100,000 a night would move through that handbook," she told the *Lexington Herald-Leader*.[110] But even then, it was as wholesome and comforting as ever. According to Barbara Harper-Bach, a cookbook author and Lexington native, it's where people like her father preferred to eat instead of home. She went for the first time in the 1960s. "I immediately knew why my dad loved the food at Rogers' Restaurant so much," she said. "It was like what my grandmother and mother cooked, but more things they couldn't get regularly like the fried oysters and shrimp baskets that were out of this world." [111] They were also one of the last remaining restaurants to serve lamb fries (testicles)—if that was your thing—and "killed lettuce,"[112] an Appalachian special of lettuce wilted in a hot bacon grease dressing.

Lexington changed in the 81 years Rogers' Restaurant was opened. It was always a cosmopolitan point in its surroundings, a place poet Jonathan Espy in 1806 compared to Philadelphia, and described as, "equal in beauty and fertility to anything the imagination can paint."[113] However, toward the end of the 20th century, Lexington faced a question that affected hundreds of towns across the country—how do you serve a new, urban population while keeping your character and identity? The population nearly doubled between 1970 and 1980, Rogers' warehouse neighborhood was redeveloped, things modernized. The *Lexington Herald-Leader* said Rogers' was "surrounded—and eventually strangled by—an ocean of new Lexington." Their Appalachian specialties no longer held their appeal. In its time, though, Rogers' demonstrated how home cooking can tie a community together. You can still get home cooking at home, but places like Rogers' were homes for everyone.

ROGERS' SALMON CROQUETTES

The salmon croquettes with tartar sauce come up in multiple remembrances of Rogers' Restaurant as a standard of the menu, a weekly favorite that was always anticipated. The salmon gets bite from the lemon juice and celery salt, and the white sauce adds a soft creaminess, a pairing as natural as lox and cream cheese.

SERVES 4

THICK WHITE SAUCE

2 tbsp (28 g) butter

2 tbsp (16 g) all-purpose flour

2 cups (473 ml) whole milk

Salt and red pepper to taste

CROQUETTES

2 cups (480 g) canned salmon, drained and boned

2 cups (473 ml) thick white sauce (recipe above)

½ tsp salt

1 tsp (5 ml) lemon juice

1 egg yolk, beaten

¼ tsp celery salt

1 egg

2 tbsp (30 ml) water

1 cup (240 g) crushed saltine crackers

Crisco, for frying

Rogers' Tartar Sauce (page 115) and lemon slices, to serve

To make the white sauce, melt the butter in a small saucepan over medium heat. Add the flour and stir together for 4 to 5 minutes, until it turns golden. Slowly whisk in the milk, little by little until it's fully incorporated. Add the salt and red pepper to taste. Cook until the sauce has thickened, a few more minutes, then remove from heat.

Mix together the salmon, white sauce, salt, lemon juice, egg yolk and celery salt and form into cone shapes, about an inch (2.5 cm) wide at the base. Beat the other egg with the water. Dip each croquette into the cracker crumbs, into the egg wash and then into the cracker crumbs again. Arrange on a baking sheet and chill for 3 to 4 hours.

Heat enough Crisco to submerge the croquettes in a deep skillet until it reachers 385°F (196°C). Deep fry the croquettes in Crisco for about 2 minutes, or until golden brown. Drain on paper towels and serve with tartar sauce and lemon slices.

[114] For reference information see Endnotes.

Rogers' Tartar Sauce

*"I remember when the lady at Rogers' gave me this recipe she said the green onions got tangled up in the blender,"
said Barbara Harper-Bach, but luckily now the food processor will take care of that problem. This thick
tartar sauce was remembered by many. The secret ingredient? Miracle Whip.*

SERVES 4

2 tbsp (30 g) green onions

2 tbsp (30 g) fresh parsley

2 small green olives, pitted

1 cup (236 ml) Miracle Whip

Place the onions, parsley and olives in a food processor to chop fine, but don't purée. (Alternately, chop fine by hand). Add the Miracle Whip and mix until thoroughly combined. Serve with salmon croquettes, or your favorite seafood.

CLIFTON'S CAFETERIA

Los Angeles, CA
1931-2011

———·——

Clifton's motto was "No Check Too Small," which was probably easy to live by in 1931. The Great Depression had potential customers more concerned about eating at all than eating out, and yet here appeared a chain that almost insisted on not making a profit. Each check displayed the exact cost of food and service, plus one cent for profit. However, guests were encouraged to pay whatever they felt was right. "We really mean that regardless of prices or what figure your check comes to—We want you to pay just what you please," explained The Clifton Tray, the cafeteria's weekly pamphlet. "If you feel you would come here—but on account of this or that price—you cannot—Why, bless your heart—This we fail to accept graciously—You owe us nothing—or for any reasons you have an unpleasant visit."[115]

Clifton's Cafeteria, "The Cafeterias of the Golden Rule," was founded by Cliff Clinton, the son of a Salvation Army Captain and a devout Christian. The food was standard cafeteria "comfort food" fare— hearty bean soups, casseroles and fruit pies—served surrounded by decor meant to evoke the woods of the Santa Cruz mountains. It featured "a rock garden, with jagged, protruding boulders, dozens of waterfalls and babbling brooks, tumbling down over the [tables], various green plants and tropical palms, growing natural—and concealed neon lights, giving the entire scene an almost theatrical effect."[116]

Clifton's was not just a restaurant, but an experience in Clinton's idea of clean living. Clinton immersed himself in Los Angeles politics, railing against corrupt politicians and organized crime, and The Clifton Tray featured health tips, poetry, philosophy, but also the occasional political rant, or endorsement of a candidate Clinton believed would do away with Los Angeles cronyism. It also alerted customers to everything their check was funding. The restaurant was the center of a small empire Clinton was building, from job search services to the "Penny Coveteria," where those in need could eat for one cent a dish. "We will operate it as long as a need exists," explained The Clifton Tray, "We must feed our hungry folks without delay or red tape." Later, Clinton would found Meals for Millions, a non-profit focused on distributing food to starving people around the world.

Though much was said about the mission behind Clifton's Cafeterias, not much was mentioned about the food—other than that it was cheap. The food at Clifton's was meant to fill those who needed it, with meat, pies and stews adorning the menu. They'd serve free birthday cakes, and roast beef and turkey on Thanksgiving. Still, the food was unique. One diner mentioned "beets in sweet and sour sauce," a rich chocolate cream cake and "the best round of roast beef."[117] His verdict? "Exceptional cafeteria dining. Consistently top-notch food and service."

Even if you didn't need to frequent the Penny Coveteria, it seemed difficult to spend money at Clifton's. In 1942, they offered afternoon meals of "a soup, spaghetti and meatballs, two vegetables, sherbet and tea or coffee for five cents."[118] If you couldn't afford the five cents, you could get it for free, a slightly confusing offer considering you could eat for free anyway at any other time if you chose. However, not many did—according to The Tray, just 1.5 percent of the customers ever chose to dine for free. At Clifton's Brookdale, the downtown LA location that opened in 1935, that meant just 150 people of the average 10,000 customers a day in the 1940s didn't pay.

At its peak, the chain consisted of eight locations, each designed differently and serving different menus, but each adhering to the Golden Rule. However, Cliff Clinton died in 1969, and beginning in the 1980s, various locations began closing. In 2011 the family sold the remaining Brookdale location, which was closed for remodeling. It reopened in 2015, with the same kitschy decor, a new Tiki bar and without the beloved Golden Rule (though certainly with charitable intentions). But it will have a bit of a sordid story to take with it into the future. In 2013, Ray Richmond wrote an article for *LA Weekly*[119] about disposing of his mother's ashes in the walls of Clifton's Brookdale. The reason? His mother was Cliff Clinton's longtime mistress, and it was his way of helping them reunite. Even the most virtuous men have their secrets.

CLIFTON'S FRUIT NUT TORTE

This sticky fruitcake is emblematic of the kind of food served at Clifton's—just elaborate enough to make it special, but not so much that it ceases to be comfortable and familiar. That's probably due to ingredients like fruit cocktail and evaporated milk that are available to any home cook.

SERVES 8

1 egg

1 cup (236 ml) fruit cocktail in juice, undrained

1 cup (201 g) granulated sugar

1 cup (128 g) all-purpose flour, sifted

1 tsp (5 g) baking soda

¼ tsp salt

½ cup (120 g) chopped walnuts

¼ cup (55g) brown sugar

½ cup (120 g) evaporated milk

½ cup (113 g) butter

½ tsp vanilla extract

Whipped cream to serve

Preheat the oven to 350°F (176°C). Beat together the egg, fruit cocktail and ¼ cup (50 g) granulated sugar. Stir in the flour, baking soda and salt and mix thoroughly. Pour into greased 9-inch (22.8-cm) round pan. Combine the walnuts and brown sugar, and sprinkle on top of batter. Bake for 30 minutes.

For the icing, combine the rest of the granulated sugar, evaporated milk and butter. Bring to a boil in a small saucepan, and boil for 3 minutes, stirring. Remove from heat and add the vanilla. Pour the hot icing over the cake as it comes out of the oven. Serve with whipped cream.

[120] For reference information see Endnotes.

CLIFTON'S JAMOCHA SAUCE

Flavors of banana, rum and coffee give this rich chocolate sauce a light, fruity twist. It works well on anything from vanilla ice cream to rum cake.

MAKES 1³/₄ CUPS (415 ML)

1 cup (236 ml) dark corn syrup

¼ cup (60 ml) chocolate syrup

½ cup (110 g) brown sugar, packed

1 tsp (5 g) instant coffee powder

½ tsp vanilla extract

½ tsp rum

Scant ⅛ tsp banana extract

Heat together the syrups, sugar and coffee until the sugar and coffee are completely dissolved. Remove from heat and add the vanilla extract, rum and banana extract. Mix until fully incorporated. Serve warm, or let cool and store in an airtight container in the refrigerator.

[121] For reference information see Endnotes.

CLIFTON'S ZUCCHINI MONTEREY

Another simple dish from Clifton's, this vegetarian casserole works excellently as either a side dish or a main course.
The spices and peppers keep it from becoming bland zucchini mush, as do the crispy bread crumbs on top.
Plus, you can't go wrong with a ton of cheese.

SERVES 8

1.3 lb (595 g) zucchini, cubed 1-inch (2.5-cm) square

4 eggs, slightly beaten

½ cup (118 ml) milk

½ tsp MSG

1 tsp (5 g) salt

Pinch cayenne pepper

2 tbsp (30 g) baking powder

3 tbsp (24 g) all-purpose flour

¼ cup (60 g) fresh parsley, chopped

½ cup (120 g) green chili peppers, diced

3 tbsp (45 g) pimentos, diced

1 lb (453 g) jack cheese, grated

1½ tsp (7 ml) vegetable oil

⅓ cup (80 g) bread crumbs

3 tsp (15 g) butter

Preheat the oven to 350°F (176°C). Steam the zucchini until slightly tender. Combine the eggs, milk, MSG, salt, cayenne pepper, baking powder, flour and parsley in a large bowl, and mix to remove lumps. Add the chili peppers, pimentos and cheese, and stir well. Add the steamed, drained zucchini and stir gently. Oil a 1½ quart (1.4 L) casserole dish and dust with half of the bread crumbs. Pour in the zucchini mixture, and sprinkle the remaining bread crumbs lightly on top. Dot with butter. Bake for 55 minutes, until top is golden brown.

[122] For reference information see Endnotes.

HENRY THIELE'S

Portland, OR

1932-1995

If you've heard the name Henry Thiele and you don't live in Portland, it's likely because of James Beard. The iconic chef was so fond of Thiele's German pancakes that he included the recipe in *American Cookery*, saying only that Henry Thiele's restaurant "made a great specialty of these pancakes." But Thiele cuts a much larger figure in Portland's culinary history than Beard lets on.

Henry Thiele (sometimes styled Henri) was born in Germany in 1882, and after immigrating to America in 1893, began working his way across kitchens in America. Beginning at the Waldorf Astoria in New York, he was eventually lured to Portland by Simon Benson, a lumber baron and philanthropist. He opened the Columbia Gorge Hotel near Hood River in 1921 and made Thiele the head chef. He also worked at Benson's Hotel Oregon in Portland, where Benson's son would hang out with his friend, James Beard, whose mother owned a boarding house down the street. The two would reportedly spend hours in the hotel's kitchen, watching Thiele cook.[123] In 1932, Thiele branched out, and built a prominent building in downtown Portland that became his own Henry Thiele's. Eventually, he expanded his empire throughout Oregon, as did his son, who ran a restaurant of the same name on the Oregon coast. He even ran a restaurant concession at the Portland Assembly Center, a Japanese detention camp that operated for a few months in 1942.[124]

Thiele infused his German heritage into much of his French cuisine. "I remember meeting a friend there who foisted on me my first Dutch Baby, the big fluffy pancakes with powdered sugar," said Richard Engeman, a Pacific Northwest food historian. "And for a while I worked down the street at a deli called Rose's, and to get something different we'd go up to Henry Thiele's and gobble up 35-cent Princess Charlotte puddings." As traditional as some of these dishes were, Thiele also had a mind for innovation. In 1917, potatoes were 4½ cents a pound, sending some into a frenzy over the high cost. Thiele came up with a recipe for potato substitute. In his letter to the Rotary Club, where this substitute was served, he warned of the dangers of food waste—a premonition of the farm-to-ta-ble restaurant trends that dominate modern-day Portland. "I could charge one-third less," he wrote, "if we were able to reduce our portions and not give the variety, which is the cause of our greatest expense."

His mind for simplicity and quality was apparent in his restaurant, a stable place in a changing dining world. In the 1930s, in the midst of a Depression, most people dining out cared about cost over quality. As prohibition ended and the economy picked up, it became more about the experience—and the liquor. Going out was going to dine and dance, drink some cocktails and have a whole night. But "Thiele's is always a sedate place," said Engeman, where food was always the focus over alcohol.

Thiele died in 1952, and his second wife, Margaret, continued to operate the restaurant until selling it in 1990. There was no line of succession to carry it on, and Portland had a culinary mecca to become. But Thiele was representative not just of Portland's food history, but the changing ideas about what chefs could be—not just practicers of a trade, but influencers and celebrities. "[Young people] have been taught to look upon the cooking trade as very minor and undesirable work," he said in 1917. "It should be put differently before them. . .He must first learn to love it, before he can produce wholesome food."

HENRY THIELE'S BRATWURST AND SWEET AND SOUR LENTILS

The sweet-and-sour lentils elevate this dish from typical meat-and-potatoes fare to something that demonstrates how Henry Thiele made such a name for himself. It combines French and German influences into a distinctly American dish.

SERVES 4

2 cups (480 g) brown lentils

Ham stock (optional)

¾ tsp seasoned salt

2 onions

5 strips bacon, finely diced

3 tbsp (24 g) all-purpose flour

¼ cup (55g) brown sugar

¼ cup (60 ml) white wine vinegar

1 medium apple, diced

4 bratwurst

2 tbsp (28 g) butter

Soak the lentils in cold water for 2 hours. Drain, then cover the lentils with water or ham stock by an inch in a small saucepan. Add the seasoned salt, and simmer until three-quarters done, about 15 to 20 minutes. Drain the lentils, retaining the liquid. Sauté one onion, finely diced and bacon over medium high heat until the onion is translucent and the fat has rendered from the bacon, about 10 minutes. Whisk in the flour, then add the liquid from the simmered lentils, sugar and vinegar and cook until reduced and thickened, about 15 minutes. Add the apple and lentils and simmer slowly until lentils are tender, about another 5 to 10 minutes.

For the bratwurst, cover with water in a saucepan and steam for about 10 minutes, being sure not to let the water boil. Remove, and sauté with butter and remaining onion, sliced, until light brown. Serve with lentils.

[125] For reference information see Endnotes.

HENRY THIELE'S BÉARNAISE SAUCE

"I have ingested some pretty miserable versions of béarnaise sauce in various and sundry restaurants over the years," wrote James Beard in 1983. The recipe he claims to have used for himself came form Henry Thiele, which Beard tried as a young chef. It was "love at first bite," the secret being "fresh French tarragon." The sauce can be served over nearly anything, from grilled chicken to lamb chops to fish.

MAKES 1 CUP (237 ML)

½ cup (118 ml) dry white wine

4 shallots, finely sliced

2 tbsp (30 g) fresh tarragon

8 tbsp (113 g) unsalted butter

4 egg yolks

Salt to taste

Reduce the white wine, shallots and tarragon in a saucepan over medium heat, until there is a thick glaze at the bottom of the saucepan, being sure not to let it burn. In a separate pan, melt the butter until it begins to bubble. In a large bowl beat together the egg yolks, then add the wine glaze and the butter, beating until it's thickened and emulsified, almost the consistency of mayonnaise (this can be done in the food processor). Season with salt and serve.

[126] For reference information see Endnotes.

Henry Thiele, in the preparation of his menu selects only the choicest of merchandise with emphasis upon service and cleanliness. National dishes of all countries are prepared, as well as a variety of his own specials. The culinary departments are open to inspection at all times and Henry Thiele welcomes suggestions for the improvement of each. The gourmet will find at Henry's the food and service that his discriminating taste demands.

TWENTY THIRD AT BURNSIDE, PORTLAND, OREGON

Henry Thiele's Potato Substitute

Henry Thiele first served this substitute for potatoes at a Rotary Club luncheon, and the Oregon Daily Journal reported it was "found appetizing." Potato prices were rising, but Chef Henry claimed he could produce four pounds (1.8 kg) of this potato substitute with just one pound (454 g) of flour. It's a fun experiment in cooking, and one that still produces delectable fries at the end.

MAKES 12 SMALL POTATOES

½ cup (113 g) dried English split peas
5 cups (1.2 L) water
2 tbsp (30 g) lard
Scant 2 cups (226 g) wheat flour
½ lb (226 g) potatoes, mashed
Salt to taste

Soak the peas for six hours in 3 cups (709 ml) of water in a small saucepan. After six hours, heat the peas and water and boil until tender, for about 20 minutes. Strain and set aside. Take 2 cups (473 ml) water with the lard and bring to boil. Slowly whisk the flour into the water and lard, and remove from heat. In a large bowl, mash together the mashed potatoes, peas, flour mixture and a little salt. Let cool, and form into 3-inch (7.5-cm) ovals. These can be dredged in flour and fried, or sliced and fried, for 3–4 minutes per side, for potato substitute french fries.

[127] For reference information see Endnotes.

BOAR & CASTLE

Greensboro, NC

1932-1980

————•——

There's always been a divide between the events of the past and the patina nostalgia can cast over them. Were our childhoods the way we remember them, or do they just seem that much more magical preserved in our memory's amber? Were things better then, or do we just miss how we think it was? If we were young again, would we gravitate toward the same things, or are we just products of our time?

Places like the Boar & Castle seem to naturally stir questions like these. When asked what the Greensboro, North Carolina, drive-in was like, most people who remembered it came up with the same answer: *American Graffiti*. The Boar & Castle certainly had all the elements you'd imagine a mid-century teenage hangout to have: it was a place to eat burgers and fries, a place to see and be seen, and maybe a place to make out with your partner. "The young people would cruise through there," said Don Coble, who worked at the Boar & Castle as a teenager. "On the right side of the restaurant they had these vines, and it was sort of like a lovers lane. People still blush about that."[128] By all accounts it was exactly the burger joint we were sold in the movies.

The Boar & Castle was first opened as a sit-down restaurant by Leon Thomas in 1932,[129] but teenage car culture made it clear that brisk business could be done by a drive-in. Through the mid-20th century, the Boar & Castle became a popular fixture in Greensboro, and Coble remembers just about everyone in town made a point to stop by, especially given that there weren't many other places in the area that made it easy to just hang out. But it wasn't just the atmosphere—"people just liked the food." They served nothing that complicated—burgers, onion rings, a butter steak sandwich that Coble still gets requests to make at reunions—but the key ingredient was the Boar & Castle sauce, the recipe of which came from Thomas's mother. Not quite ketchup, not quite BBQ sauce and not quite Worcestershire, it smothered nearly everything on the menu, and was just one more thing that kept locals coming back.

In 1980 the restaurant closed; its iconic castle-shaped building torn down and replaced by an insurance office building. "Today they would never have torn it down," says Coble, "it probably would have been a historic site." James Ennis, the restaurant's manager, continued to bottle the famous sauce, which is still available in the Carolinas today. Della Gray, who has recently taken over Boar & Castle sauce duties, recalls, "I was setting up a display at a grocery store in Roanoke, VA, and this woman was watching me, and she started crying. After a while I asked if she was okay, and she said 'My mama was at the Boar & Castle the day WW II ended, and this reminds me of her.'"

A deep nostalgia can be heard in the voice of anyone who speaks of the Boar & Castle. It has inspired the kind of loyalty reserved for sports teams and alma maters, with fan clubs still gathering to share memories and photographs. Modernity is blamed for the Castle's demise, whether in the form of fast-food chains, highways or teenagers who'd rather play video games than cruise the night with their friends. The truth is we can't know if people would have valued a place like the Boar & Castle the same way today, but maybe that's not the point. Maybe the point is that it's still being valued.

Boar & Castle's Butter Steak Sandwich

What makes this sandwich taste so good? Butter. More butter than you think you should probably consume, but this is drive-in food. This recipe was remembered by Don Coble, who worked at the Boar & Castle as a teenager. The butter-griddled beef is what sends you back to the diner counter or the drive-in. The Boar & Castle served this sandwich with their proprietary sauce, flavored with mustard, tomato and anchovy, but use good quality beef and it'll hardly need it.

SERVES 2

½ lb (226 g) beef rump roast, sliced ½-inch (1.25-cm) thick

4 tbsp (60 g) butter, divided

2 hamburger buns

Pound out the beef until it's ¼-inch (6-mm) thick (this will help tenderize the meat). Heat 2 tablespoons (30 g) butter in a large skillet over high heat. Cook the beef in the butter, coating it on all sides and being sure not to overcook. As it's cooking, place the sandwich rolls on the griddle with a ½ tablespoon (7.5 g) of butter in each until crispy and golden, about 5 minutes. Serve the beef in a roll topped with butter.

[130] For reference information see Endnotes.

BOAR & CASTLE'S JELLY ROLL

*Don Coble says to use something similar to seedless BBQ Bread for this recipe, which he remembers
the Boar & Castle serving for breakfast. You can't go wrong with a griddle roll toasted in butter,
and as the strawberry jam melts with the butter, you can see why it became a popular item.*

SERVES 4

4 rolls of BBQ Bread

4 tbsp (60 g) butter

Strawberry jam

Dip both sides of a roll of BBQ Bread in melted butter, and cook on a hot griddle
until crispy and golden, about 5–7 minutes. Slice open and fill with strawberry jam.

[131] For reference information see Endnotes.

PERINO'S

Los Angeles, CA
1932-1986

In an obituary in the *Los Angeles Times* in 1982,[132] Alexander Perino was called "the man who set the standards." His restaurant, Perino's, was known as a place that refused to cut corners, a quirk made remarkable given that it opened in the midst of the Depression, and in a Los Angeles that was more hustlers and gangsters than glitz and glamour. Perino, an immigrant from the Piedmonte region of Italy, borrowed $2,000 to open his restaurant in 1932, and at the time his had the highest prices in town.

But people came; first gangsters, then the stars like Mae West and Bette Davis, then reviewers from New York, who were still wary about giving restaurants on the West Coast the time of day. For a while it was a beacon of "civilization" in a western city that still felt wild. That civilization came from the "continental"-style menu so favored at the time, as Americans were not yet ready for a high-end restaurant that didn't serve Delmonico steaks and shrimp cocktail. Today, Perino's menu[133] looks hectic and disorganized, imported Russian caviar and vichyssoise served along frogs legs almandine or gnocchi pietmontese. But there were Italian notes in nearly every dish. One memorable appetizer was simple slices of pumpernickel bread coated with butter and Parmesan cheese. Places like Perino's began to convince diners that Italian flavors belonged at the upscale tables, because even if the food was foreign, no one could argue with the quality.

Perino, and his chef Atillio Bolzano, became notorious for their attention to detail. Tomatoes were never kept on ice, mayonnaise from the bottle was never used and no meat was ever frozen. "People call and want a gourmet dinner for $15," Perino told *Redlands Daily Facts* in 1970,[134] "You can't even begin to do that. With the proper wines a gourmet dinner might be $50 a person."

More than the food or the clientele, the main attraction was Alex Perino himself, who stayed personally involved in every aspect of the restaurant's operation. "When I was about 8 years old, my grandfather was home sick with the flu," said Del Banks,[135] whose grandfather worked at the restaurant. "Alex made a special trip to bring him some soup that chef Atillio Bolzano had made for him. On the way, he stopped by our house and hand delivered a cheesecake to my mother." He also recalls a day his grandfather surprised him at school with a lunch from Perino's for his whole class, and his teachers stood in awe as he told them how he ate like that all the time. "It wasn't until I was older that I realized that I was eating Delmonico steaks, strip steaks, pheasant, squab, filet mignon and duck a l'orange. It was a good life!"

Technically, the restaurant lasted until 1986, but it began its decline in 1969, when Perino was forced to sell the restaurant. He remained as president for a time, but eventually left, with Bolzano and much of the staff following him. He could see the changes coming. He complained about the lack of "passion" he found in new employees, and younger clientele who no longer valued the starched tablecloths and quality food. To put it bluntly, "It's a dinosaur," said one bankruptcy court trustee on the day of Perino's last dinner. Also, by 1970, Perino's was no longer the only game in town. Los Angeles was no longer a curiosity of the West Coast, but a world-class city that was only attracting more restaurateurs.

If anything, it was Perino's attention to quality that made longevity an uphill battle. "A restaurant of this type can never make any money," he said. "You make a living, yes, but not money." At least he never compromised.

PERINO'S SHRIMP SALAD

Thousand Island dressing has gotten a bad rap over the years, but the version served with this salad is fresher and has more bite than anything that comes out of a bottle. In the true Perino spirit, quality is key for this simple salad. Hothouse tomatoes and under-ripe avocado just won't do.

SERVES 2

½ avocado, sliced

Hearts of romaine

1 beefsteak tomato, peeled and cut in wedges

½ lb (226 g) large shrimp, cooked

Pimiento for garnish

THOUSAND ISLAND DRESSING

1 cup (236 ml) mayonnaise

½ cup (118 ml) ketchup

½ green bell pepper, diced

2 sweet gherkin pickles, diced

1 tbsp (15 g) pimiento, diced

¼ onion, diced

Chill all the ingredients (Perino advised all the serving dishes should be chilled as well). Fan the slices of avocado over a bed of hearts of romaine. Surround the fanned avocado with wedges of tomato, and border with shrimp, cut in half lengthwise. Garnish the salad with a whole shrimp and a ribbon of pimiento. Serve with Thousand Island dressing. To make the dressing, whisk together all the ingredients until smooth and fully encorporated.

[136] For reference information see Endnotes.

PERINO'S CHICKEN LORENZO SALAD

Chicken Lorenzo Salad was a "specialty" of Perino's, showcasing the restaurant's reputation for fresh food and continental style. Serve with thin slices of pumpernickel bread buttered and topped with Parmesan cheese, another Perino's specialty, for a real taste of what a luncheon there would have been like.

SERVES 2

1 breast of chicken

¼ cup (60 g) carrot, chopped

¼ onion, chopped

1 stalk of celery, chopped

¼ cup (60 g) parsley, chopped

2 anchovy filets, chopped

¼ hard boiled egg, chopped

¼ tomato, chopped

½ head iceberg lettuce

LORENZO DRESSING

1 tbsp (15 ml) red wine vinegar

3 tbsp (44 ml) olive oil

1 tbsp (15 ml) ketchup

Salt and pepper to taste

2 tbsp (30 g) watercress, chopped

Black olives, for garnish

Bring a small saucepan full of water to a boil. Add the chicken, carrot, onion, celery and parsley and boil until the chicken is cooked through, about 20 minutes. Let it cool in the broth.

Cut the chicken breast into ½-inch (1.3-cm) pieces, and mix with the anchovy, hard-boiled egg and tomato in a large bowl. Save two lettuce leaves for the garnish, and chop the rest of the lettuce into bite-sized pieces and mix with the rest of the salad.

For the dressing, whisk together the vinegar, olive oil, ketchup and salt and pepper, and add the watercress at the very end. Toss the salad with dressing until just coated. Lay reserved lettuce leaves on a serving platter and pile the salad in the middle. Garnish with black olives.

[137] For reference information see Endnotes.

CHARLIE'S CAFE EXCEPTIONALE

Minneapolis, MN
1933-1982

———— · ————

"Sumptuous" is the word Jack Kabrud, curator at the Hennepin History Museum, used to describe Charlie's Cafe Exceptionale. It had many of the trappings of most high-end restaurants in mid-century America—crystal chandeliers, lush carpets, oak paneling. "Everything was quiet, and there was a dignity there. It made it all the more special." Taken at just its component parts, Charlie's Cafe Exceptionale seems almost ordinary, but great restaurants are rarely just the sum of their parts.

Two Charlies are responsible for Charlie's Cafe Exceptionale. The first is Charles Saunders, a pilot who was rumored to have been a bootlegger before opening the restaurant in 1933, the year prohibition ended. And post-prohibition dining was all about sumptuousness, taking the secret indulgences of the 1920s public. That's where the other Charles came in. Charles "The Finn" Herlin immigrated to America from Finland in 1893, and was responsible for the restaurant's cocktail menu, which included his President cocktail. Herlin's version, a combination of gin and citrus juices, was a signature part of his repertoire, and he'd bottle the ingredients for other bartenders to use, just so no one would steal his recipe. When he died in 1933, shortly after the restaurant opened, he hadn't told any of the bartenders what was actually in his mix. They approximated, but the original recipe died with Herlin.[138]

Saunders continued without Herlin, eventually moving the restaurant across the street to a two-story English Tudor-style building constructed explicitly for the restaurant. It was even more luxurious than the original restaurant, with a wrought-iron staircase, hand-painted murals, and an on-site butcher shop. Outside, a bronze statue of a nude woman was erected, nicknamed the "Scherzo." The statue was made by artist Harriet Frishmuth, and originally stood in the garden court of the Foshay Tower, obscured from most public view. Once she moved to Charlie's street corner, she became a point of moral concern. Saunders refused to cover the Scherzo up, but it soon became a tradition every spring for local nurses to dress her up in a nurse uniform.

These aesthetic details all contributed to Charlie's becoming a fixture of the Minneapolis fine-dining scene. "There were a number of really fine restaurants in Minneapolis through the 1950s and 1960s," said Kabrud, "but few that were of the same caliber as Charlie's." But it was a product of its time. A 1953 clip from the *Minneapolis Spokesman*[139] reports how the restaurant "evicted Frank W. Fager, executive secretary of the Minneapolis Mayor's Council on Human Relations bodily when he objected to being refused a reservation service because he was in the company of Clifford Rucker, a Negro and executive secretary of the Governor's Interracial Commission." At that time, the only black person to dine in the main dining room had been William Seabron, of the Urban League, who dined with Mayor Hubert Humphrey. The paper reported "Saunders from that day was anti-Humphrey."

By 1959, Saunders had married Louise Herou, and when he died of a heart attack in 1964, Louise took over operations of Charlie's. "She gave it her signature as well," said Kabrud, and though she had no restaurant experience (she received her J.D. in 1950), it became nationally known under her guidance. The food was simple, upscale, prepared with precision, exhibiting as much French influence as Minnesotan Nordic. Menus boasted "traditional lutefisk" around the winter holidays, baked pheasant with Minnesota wild rice, and roast peppered rib-eye. Their most famous dish was, of all things, potato salad, the recipe of which was closely held by Louise Saunders. And while the potato salad was certainly a far cry from what you'd find at a Memorial Day picnic, you wonder how much had to do with the actual potato salad and how much was the venue.

Unlike many famous restaurants, who coast on their reputation until they fizzle out, Charlie's "never lost a bit of its reputation, right up to the very end," according to Kabrud. Instead, it was the neighborhood that was changing. When Charlie's opened they were on the outskirts of downtown Minneapolis, but by 1982 downtown had grown, with skyscrapers obscuring the two-story restaurant, and plenty of new options for the city's well-off. Louise Saunders sold the building, which was razed and replaced by a gleaming glass tower, and she turned down the offer to reopen Charlie's in the building's lobby, saying she would rather people remember it as it was. "It was mournful," said Kabrud. "A lot of people were disappointed to see Charlie's go."

The individual parts of Charlie's dispersed. A few recipes were re-created by different restaurants. The bar was removed and re-created at the nearby Monte Carlo Cafe. Its name is now invoked at a local food and restaurant awards ceremony. It lives on in pieces, which is better than not living on at all.

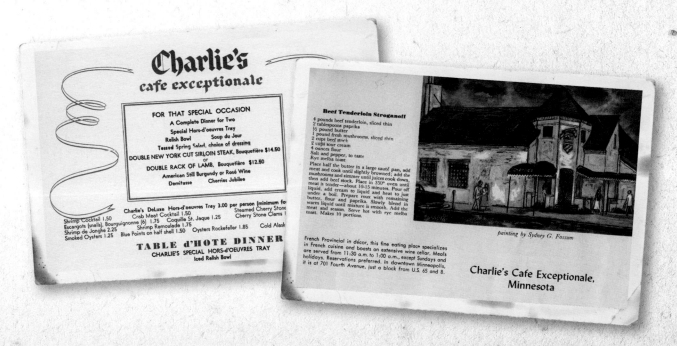

CHARLIE'S CAFE EXCEPTIONALE
ROAST PEPPERED RIB EYE OF BEEF

A simple roast beef is something that doesn't need to be messed with much, but if you want to add a little more flavor, Charlie's combination of cardamom and soy sauce elevate this dish from a regular Midwestern beef roast to something extravagant.

SERVES 8

———— ·· ————

1 (6 lb [2.7 kg]) boneless rib eye

½ cup (120 g) coarsely ground black pepper

½ tsp ground cardamom

1 cup (236 ml) soy sauce

¾ cup (177 ml) white wine vinegar

1 tbsp (15 g) tomato paste

1 tsp (5 g) paprika

½ tsp garlic powder

Trim the rib eye of excess fat. Combine the black pepper and cardamom and spread thoroughly over meat, pressing into the meat with your hands. Combine the soy sauce, vinegar, tomato paste, paprika and garlic powder in a deep dish, and marinate the crusted rib eye in the mixture for 24 hours, turning occasionally if it is not completely submerged.

Preheat the oven to 300°F (149°C). Gently remove the rib eye from marinade, being sure to keep the crust intact, and wrap tightly in aluminum foil. Place it in a roasting pan and bake for 2 hours for medium rare. Open the foil and pour out and reserve the drippings. Raise the oven temperature to 350°F (176°C) and return the roast to the oven, uncovered, to brown. Meanwhile, strain the drippings and skim the fat, add to equal parts water and boil until thickened. Serve the rib eye sliced with au jus.

[140] For reference information see Endnotes.

CHARLIE'S POTATO SALAD

There exist many recipes for Charlie's famed potato salad, though Louise Saunders always claimed to hold the recipe close. This version was given to Better Homes & Gardens *by the restaurant in the 1960s. Creamy, with bits of crunch and spice, it's easy to see how Charlie's customers would have become obsessed. If possible, make your own mayonnaise as Charlie's surely did, for even more flavor.*

SERVES 8

5 medium potatoes, pared and freshly cooked

1 tsp (5 g) salt

A dash white pepper

2 tbsp (30 g) green onions, chopped

3 hard boiled eggs, diced

2 tbsp (30 g) pimiento, chopped

1¼ cup (295 ml) mayonnaise

¼ cup (60 g) diced celery

Dice the potatoes and sprinkle them with salt and pepper. In a large bowl, combine the potatoes, green onions, eggs, pimiento, mayonnaise and celery. Gently fold everything together, being sure not to break up the eggs or potatoes too much. Add more salt and pepper to taste if needed. Chill for 2 hours before serving.

[142] For reference information see Endnotes.

CHARLIE'S PRESIDENT COCKTAIL

The original President cocktail may have died with Charles "The Finn" Herlin, but this recipe found in notes from the restaurant at the Hennepin County Library kept customers happy for many years. The dash of grenadine adds color and just a touch of sweetness while not turning it into something entirely tropical.

MAKES 2 COCKTAILS

1½ oz (44 ml) orange juice

1½ oz (44 ml) lemon juice

1½ oz (44 ml) gin

1 dash grenadine

Ice

Combine the ingredients in a shaker and stir until cold. Strain into a martini glass and serve.

[141] For reference information see Endnotes.

CHARLIE'S OYSTER DRESSING

This recipe appeared in a pamphlet entitled "Holiday Recipes," printed by Charlie's Café, a traditional holiday stuffing made lighter by the use of rice in place of bread. It can be enjoyed on its own, or used to stuff any roast poultry.

SERVES 6

1 tbsp (15 g) butter

1 medium onion, diced

2 garlic cloves, minced

½ lb (226 g) pork sausage

18 oysters, shucked

12 cups (2.8 L) white rice, cooked

¼ cup (60 g) chopped parsley

⅛ tsp oregano

⅛ tsp sage

Salt and pepper to taste

Melt the butter over medium heat in a large skillet. Add the onion and garlic and cook until the onion softens and turns translucent, about 10 minutes. Remove the sausage casings and crumble the sausage into the pan. Cook until the sausage is nearly cooked through, then add the oysters and cook for another 5 minutes. In a separate bowl, combine the rice, parsley, oregano, sage, salt and pepper. Add the sausage mixture into the rice and mix thoroughly. Serve, or use as stuffing.

[143] For reference information see Endnotes.

CHASEN'S

West Hollywood, CA

1936-1995

How could a BBQ joint become "the" place for Academy Awards after parties? How could a restaurant last into the 1990s without taking credit cards? How could an actor create a place that the *New Yorker* said "meant to Hollywood what Maxim's has to Paris and '21' to New York"?[144] The *New Yorker* would know—founding editor, Harold Ross, funded the place.

The story goes that Harold Ross found Dave Chasen, a Russian immigrant turned vaudeville comedian, to be a better cook than he was an actor, and told him if he ever wanted to get out of show business, he'd help him get his start. In 1936 Chasen and his wife took that offer, and opened Chasen's Southern Pit Barbecue, a six-stool restaurant serving the chili and ribs that had already enchanted Ross. First writers came, both from Hollywood and the Algonquin scene in New York, and directors like Frank Capra (at whose house Chasen apparently mastered his rib recipe). Then came actors, then the Academy Awards parties, and the celebrity stories that sustained it. Elizabeth Taylor asking for the chili while on set for *Cleopatra*. Ronald Reagan proposing to Nancy in one of the leather booths.[145] Bob Hope riding his horse into the restaurant. By this point, Chasen had expanded into a much larger space.

No matter how refined Chasen's got, it still carried its reputation as the place where the Hollywood elite could get rowdy. "It was their meeting hall, corner bar, family restaurant and club all rolled into one," wrote Ehud Yonay[146] in the *Long Beach Independent Press-Telegram*, and sometimes even more—the restaurant initially featured a barber and a steam room. Diners were nearly guaranteed to see someone famous, and if you were lucky, you could catch one of them throwing a punch. Like many of its kind, it became more about the experience than the food. The chili continued to enchant, but through the 1950s and '60s it was more about being seen eating the chili than anything else.

Also like many of its kind, Chasen's reputation fossilized. Instead of the meeting hall for an entire generation of Hollywood creatives, it became two things—chili and celebrity sightings. Its press increasingly looked backwards, fawning over the people who used to come in, the things that already happened, instead of who was there at the present. Articles devolved into lists of celebrities who had been there and the well-worn stories surrounding them—Erroll Flynn throwing punches, Jack Dempsey playing pranks,[147] Albert Hitchcock celebrating his 75th birthday. Anything else the restaurant could have been caved to these experiences, and as that generation of Hollywood began to disappear, so did Chasen's.

Dave Chasen's wife, Maude, continued to run the restaurant after he died in 1973, serving plenty of chili and nostalgia, but by 1995 when it closed, Hollywood had moved on. There were more restaurants, different celebrities and Hollywood had turned from a Wild West city into a place of business, where a burgeoning celebrity's reputation could be ruined by getting into a drunken fight at a famous restaurant. "Things were different then," said Maude in 1973. "People were more alive…I think the people themselves were more different." Or they were just less careful, though that's not necessarily a good thing.

CHASEN'S CHILI CON CARNE

A few recipes for Chasen's famous chili have been published over the years, including in various newspapers, websites and in a longer history of the restaurant. They all have slight variations, calling for everything from corn chips to apple slices to bleu cheese as a garnish. This is a straightforward version that, I think, combines all the best features from the recipe's variations. The combination of meats and fresh parsley add a depth of flavor—it's easy to see how so many became addicted.

SERVES 6

½ lb (225 g) dried pinto beans

Water

1 (28-oz [790-g]) can diced tomatoes in juice

1 large green bell pepper, chopped

2 tbsp (30 ml) vegetable oil

3 small onions, coarsely chopped

2 cloves garlic, crushed

½ cup (113 g) parsley, chopped

½ cup (113 g) butter

2 lb (900 g) beef chuck, coarsely chopped

1 lb (450 g) pork shoulder, coarsely chopped

⅓ cup (43 g) chili powder

1 tbsp (15 g) salt

1½ tsp (7.5 g) black pepper

1½ tsp (7.5 g) ground cumin

Rinse the beans under cold water, picking out the debris. Place the beans in a Dutch oven with water to cover over high heat, and bring to a boil. Boil for 2 minutes, then remove from heat, cover and let stand 1 hour before draining off the liquid.

Rinse the beans again, and add enough fresh water to cover. Bring to a boil, then reduce heat and simmer, covered, for one hour or until tender.

Stir in the tomatoes and their juice, and let simmer for 5 minutes. Meanwhile, in a large skillet over medium-high heat sauté the bell pepper in the vegetable oil for 5 minutes. Add the chopped onions and cook until tender, stirring frequently. Stir in the garlic and parsley, and then add this whole mixture to the beans. Using the same skillet, melt the butter and sauté beef and pork chuck until browned, about 7 minutes. Drain, and add the meat to the bean mixture along with the chili powder, salt, pepper, cumin and a cup (237 ml) of water.

Bring the chili to a boil, then reduce heat to simmer and cover. Let simmer for an hour, then uncover and cook another 30 minutes, or to desired consistency. Chili shouldn't be too thick—it should be somewhat liquid but not runny like soup. Skim off the excess fat and serve.

[148] For reference information see Endnotes.

THE PUMP ROOM

Chicago, IL
1938-2011, then reopened

————·————

"When Frank Sinatra makes musical references to a restaurant, you know that restaurant is big," wrote Bob Greene on the 50th anniversary of Chicago's The Pump Room.[149] In some version of "My Kind of Town (Chicago is)," Sinatra threw in a nod to the "jumpin' Pump Room." But that wasn't the only time it was immortalized in song—in his version of "Chicago (That Toddlin' Town)" he often used the lyrics: "We'll meet at the Pump Room-Ambassador East/To say the least, on shish kebab and breast of squab we will feast/And get fleeced." Perhaps the details don't matter as much now.

The Pump Room was one of many restaurants given the nickname "the most famous restaurant in the world," and it was a strong contender. It opened in 1938 in the Ambassador East Hotel under the direction of Ernie Byfield, the son of Hungarian immigrants. His father owned the Sherman House, a historic inn in the middle of Chicago, which Ernie inherited when he died, as well as The Ambassador hotel, and a plot of land upon which he and his partners constructed the Ambassador East. Ernie already had experience running a nightclub in the Sherman House, and with the opening of the Pump Room, he built on his experience of attracting ritzy clientele. One strategy was utilizing the couple-hour layover movie stars routinely had when traveling between New York and Los Angeles, in the days before direct flights between the coasts were widely available. According to *Hollywood on Lake Michigan*,[150] Byfield used this to his advantage by offering limo service from Union Station to the restaurant, where stars had just enough time to dine and be seen before catching the second leg of their travels. By the 1940s, The Pump Room was the place to be in Chicago.

The food adhered to no particular cuisine—it didn't matter where it was from as long as it tasted rich. Beluga caviar with blini were served alongside imported foie gras and Bismarck herring. Crabmeat was wrapped in bacon and served on a flaming sword, and the "Shashlik Caucasian" Sinatra sang about was a staple. Byfield once commented on the swords, "it doesn't seem to hurt the food much, and the customers like it."[151] The original 1938 menu was headed by Chef Argante Ciabattari, who later became the Chairman of the Chicago Association of Chefs de Cuisine.

The Pump Room wasn't all about the celebrities, but it was about the atmosphere. Gail Bell,[152] who grew up just outside of Chicago, remembers visiting the Pump Room with her mother when she was a teenager: "What I can't explain is the feeling of the Pump Room, it was just wonderful. It was comfortable and it was warm, but it was elegant." Once she moved into the city, she and her mother would lunch there at least once a week, getting to know all the waitstaff, and always ordering differently. And if there were leftovers, "the food would always be wrapped in a foil swan."

No, The Pump Room wasn't all about celebrities, but they certainly helped. Eventually, the advent of transcontinental air travel slowed the flow of famous patrons, and the energy seemed to go with them. In the 1970s the Pump Room was sold and the new owners auctioned off the famous decor, including the "ostrich-plumed white satin hats of the 'coffee boys,'" and five Waterford crystal chandeliers. "The Pump Room's new owners have no use for anything but its name," stated a 1976 article.[153] Locals like Bell kept going, though she admits it felt markedly different, as it had to. Now a foil swan might feel a little cheesy, a flaming sword a little awkward, and a booth reserved solely for VIPs a little classist. It remains under the same name, catering to Chicago's new elite, with a menu and an atmosphere that would be unrecognizable to Ernie Byfield. It survived, but only by changing with the times.

PUMP ROOM SHASHLIK CAUCASIAN

In 1951, the Pantagraph *published this recipe for The Pump Room's famed lamb shashlik en brochette, later known as shashlik caucasian, which was served aflame table side. The marinade almost pickles the lamb, after which it's charred with fresh vegetables and served with a complex hot sauce. In 1955, Chef Ferario suggested serving it with rice and a baked tomato, but it'd stand on its own at any backyard grill.*

SERVES 4

1¼ lb (566 g) leg of lamb (tender part), cut into ½-inch (1.25-cm) squares

Burgundy wine

Juice of 1 lemon

2 bay leaves

1 tsp (5 g) salt

1 tsp (5 g) crushed black pepper

1 tbsp (15 ml) vinegar

Tomatoes, cut into chunks

Green peppers, cut into chunks

Onions, wedged

Rum, for flaming garnish

Marinate the meat for 24 hours in the refrigerator in a mixture of the wine (enough to cover the meat), lemon juice, bay leaves, salt, pepper and vinegar. Then pour off the marinade, and skewer the chunks of lamb, alternating with chunks of tomatoes, green peppers and onions. Broil until the meat is charred but still slightly pink inside (medium), about 2 to 4 minutes per side. Remove from the broiler, and drench in high-proof rum. Light the skewers with a match and serve in flames.

[155] For reference information see Endnotes.

PUMP ROOM HOT SAUCE

This hot sauce from Chef Ferario hits every flavor note—sweet, spicy, tangy, fresh. It's the perfect accompaniment to the Shashlik Caucasian, or any grilled meat.

SERVES 4

———•———

1 cup (236 ml) chili sauce

½ cup (118 ml) ketchup

1½ tsp (7.5 g) piccalilli or sweet pepper relish

1½ tsp (7.5 ml) honey

1½ tsp (7.5 g) horseradish, grated

1½ tsp (7.5 ml) vinegar

1½ tsp (7.5 g) chopped chutney

Salt and pepper to taste

Whisk all the ingredients together in a bowl. Serve with grilled meat.

[156] For reference information see Endnotes.

PUMP ROOM CHICKEN HASH

This recipe appeared in The Prescott Courier*, apparently pulled from a never-published Pump Room cookbook manuscript, exactly as it was in the original handwritten notes. The original dish was prepared table side, and Chef Ciabattari notes that it should be served in a pie or puff pastry shell, or over fresh toast points, which makes sense given that it's essentially a lightly seasoned, creamy chicken pot pie filling. The "chicken simmered in the manner described will yield an excellent chicken soup for four for another meal—nothing to be neglected in today's economy."*

SERVES 4-6

1 chicken, about 3 lb (1.3 kg)

½ cup (100g) chopped carrots

½ cup (100g) chopped onions

½ cup (100g) chopped celery

2 bay leaves

1 tbsp (15 g) whole black peppercorns, bruised

1 clove garlic

1½ tsp (7.5 g) salt

Pinch of nutmeg

2 whole cloves

5 cups (1.2 L) water

½ cup (120 g) butter

½ cup (64 g) flour

1 cup (240 g) finely diced, blanched celery

2 egg yolks

¼ cup (60 ml) heavy cream

2 tbsp (30 ml) dry sherry or Madeira wine

Salt or pepper to taste

Cut the chicken into serving pieces and place in a large saucepan with carrots, onions, celery, bay leaves, peppercorns, garlic, salt, nutmeg, cloves and water. Cover and bring to boil over high heat. Lower heat and simmer for 40 to 45 minutes over very low heat, until you can easily remove the chicken meat from the bones. Remove the chicken and place on a tray to cool. Strain the liquid and set aside to cool, then skim the fat from the top. Discard the vegetables.

Remove the skin and bones from the chicken, then mince the meat. It should yield 3½ to 4 cups (840 to 960 g), depending on how well you pick it and how small you mince it. Pieces should not be larger than a green pea. Small shreds are all right.

In a heavy skillet, melt the butter over low heat. Then add the flour and whisk until mixture starts to bubble and turn yellow, about 10 minutes. Remove from heat and slowly whisk in 3 cups (710 ml) chicken stock, stirring constantly to avoid lumps. Return to medium heat and simmer for 4 to 5 minutes. Add the minced chicken and celery, fold in and continue simmering for another 5 minutes.

In a small bowl, mix the egg yolks with heavy cream. Fold the mixture into the chicken hash. Remove from heat and add the dry sherry or Madeira. Adjust seasoning to taste, and serve.

[154] For reference information see Endnotes.

Aunt Fanny's Cabin

Smyrna, GA
1941-1992

———

One has to be in a pretty privileged position to feel nostalgia for the antebellum South. Generations of owners of Aunt Fanny's Cabin—a popular soul food restaurant that relied on a heavy slavery theme—insisted they never glorified slavery. George Poole, the owner of Aunt Fanny's Cabin in 1982,[157] said any complaints usually came from "some Northern liberal who feels the atmosphere is degrading. So we just try to explain as we can that this is the way it's always been." Still, where is the line between honoring the past, and pretending that this was a time that anyone, especially the all-black wait staff, wanted to return to? Whether you thought Aunt Fanny's was a humorous look at the past or an offensive caricature of slave life, it didn't stop the tourists from eating their fried chicken.

Aunt Fanny's Cabin was opened by Isoline Campbell McKenna in 1941.[158] Her family had bought land in Smyrna about fifty years prior, to be used as a home for the Campbells with houses for tenant farmers. McKenna opened the Cabin initially as a general store, to sell the goods the tenant farmers made. They sold everything from canned goods and fresh eggs to the antiques that decorated the walls, and soon expanded into a full restaurant, serving dishes made by "Aunt Fanny" Williams.

There's the myth of Aunt Fanny's Cabin, and there's the reality. The myth is that the cabin was once slave quarters for a plantation, and that Fanny Williams had been born a slave on the property. She would regale any visitors with "tales of the Old South and Sherman's march through Georgia."[159] The reality is that Williams was likely born after the Civil War, though she did work as a servant for the Campbell family. She was also a powerful figure in the black community, regularly fundraising for the Wheat Street Baptist Church (which would later become heavily involved in the Civil Rights Movement) and for a nearby "Negro Hospital." The cabin hadn't even been slave quarters; it was built in the 1890s.

Williams was by all accounts an accomplished cook, and when she died in 1949, the restaurant continued to serve her dishes. Things like fresh vegetable soup and baked squash were signatures, as well as everything from fried chicken to cornbread to ham. And though when it opened Smyrna was still a sleepy suburb of Atlanta, the metropolitan area was developing at a quick pace. The population of Smyrna increased tenfold between 1930 and 1960, partially spurred by the development of the Bell Aircraft Corporation's new plant in the county, and new owners, Harvey Hester and Marjorie Bowman, to whom McKenna sold the restaurant in 1946, were quick to capitalize on the growing population.

As the former owner of the Miami Seahawks and a boxing promoter, Hester was able to quickly draw celebrities and sports icons to the restaurant, like Susan Hayward, Ty Cobb and President Jimmy Carter. Hester and Bowman also perpetuated the slave cabin myth, assuming guests far preferred the caricature of Aunt Fanny and the antebellum South to any level of truth. Unfortunately, they were right.

Reviewers seemed charmed by the pseudo-minstrelsy. "This ramshackle, dimly lighted restaurant is the delight of the Atlanta region," wrote one Californian reviewer in 1966,[160] and described how "two small Negro boys climb up on a table and do a lively, loud, heel-clog dance." Young black boys also walked around the restaurant wearing the menu on sandwich boards, and black waitresses wore calico dresses and would occasionally drop their work to sing "Dixie" and gospel songs around the piano. A promotional postcard featured the line "AUNT FANNY SAYS: 'Save your Confederate Money Folks. The South will rise again.'" Most shocking was this report:[161]

> In the kitchen, Tommy Barbour, the white manager, teases the help. "You goin' get whupped good tonight!" he says.

> "Oh, please, don' whup me tonight, Massah Tommy," Jo Anne Trimble [a waitress] says, mock-pleadingly.

Those at the restaurant claimed they were just poking fun at the past, given that they'd come so far. So the spectacle continued, because by all accounts they had the best Southern food around. Celebrities asked for it by name, and it was frequently named as having some of the best fried chicken in the South, certainly no small task. At its best, it provided warmth, hospitality and great food. In the 1980s a quarter of a million people were visiting a year, mainly "white tourists who relish the atmosphere as much as the food." Many of the black employees told newspapers they were paid and treated well.

However, as time went on the image perpetuated by Aunt Fanny's became increasingly unacceptable. Child labor laws put an end to the black boys in their sandwich board menus, and by the early '90s many customers found themselves uncomfortable with the caricatures that had been so popular before. In 1992 owner Gretna Poole auctioned the building. Even then, the report said the restaurant represented a "quaint slice of Southern history." It may not have been quaint, but places like Aunt Fanny's are just as much a part of America's history as anything else.

Aunt Fanny's Ham with Red Gravy

Ham and water is all it takes for a rich gravy to form around this simple Southern dish. Serve with grits, cornbread or any of your favorite Southern sides.

Serves 2

4 slices of Smithfield country-cured ham, ½-inch (1.25-cm) thick

Water for soaking

1½ cups (354 ml) boiling water

Soak the ham slices for least 6 hours in water. Dry on paper towels, and remove the hard, black rind. Heat a heavy skillet over medium high heat. When ready, fry the ham slices for 5 to 7 minutes per side, until they're well browned and some of the fat has started to render. Pour off all but about 3 tablespoons (44 ml) of the fat, and set the skillet back on the heat until the fat starts smoking. Add the boiling water, and scrape the stuck bits off the bottom. Boil the fat and water for 1 to 2 minutes, then pour over ham to serve.

[162] For reference information see Endnotes.

AUNT FANNY'S BAKED SQUASH

It's probably all the butter that makes this summer squash casserole so appetizing. Topped with crispy bread crumbs and with just a little sugar to enhance the squash's natural sweetness, it's the perfect side dish to any Southern supper.

SERVES 8

3 lbs (1.3 kg) yellow summer squash

½ cup (120 g) onions, chopped

2 eggs

1 tbsp (15 g) sugar

1 tsp (5 g) salt

½ tsp black pepper

10 tbsp (141 g) butter

½ cup (120 g) cracker meal or bread crumbs

Preheat the oven to 375°F (190°C)

Wash and cut the squash into about 1-inch (2.5-cm) pieces. Boil until tender, about 3 to 6 minutes, drain and then mash thoroughly. Combine the squash with onions, eggs, sugar, salt, pepper and 8 tablespoons (113 g) butter, and pour into a baking dish. Melt the remaining butter and spread on top of the squash mixture, and then sprinkle with bread crumbs.

Bake for approximately 1 hour, until the top is well browned.

[163] For reference information see Endnotes.

AUNT FANNY'S CORNBREAD

Cornbread can so quickly turn into a sweet, puffy cake, but this recipe keeps it savory and crispy.
The recipe recommends pouring the cornbread batter in "piping hot," cast-iron muffin tins. If you don't have
cast iron, you can still heat your muffin tins in the oven as it's preheating.

YIELD 12

1 egg

2 cups (473 ml) buttermilk (or 2 cups
[473 ml] whole milk and 2 tbsp
[30 ml] vinegar)

2 cups (480 g) cornmeal

1 tsp (5 g) salt

1 tsp (5 g) baking soda

4 tbsp (57 g) butter or bacon fat, melted

Butter to serve

Preheat the oven to 400°F (204 °C).

Beat the egg and buttermilk together. Sift together the cornmeal, salt and baking soda and add to egg and milk mixture. Quickly stir in the melted butter or fat, and pour into greased and heated muffin tins about ¼-inch (0.6 cm) deep. Bake for 20 minutes until well browned. Serve with lots of butter.

[164] For reference information see Endnotes.

DEARING'S

Cleveland, OH

1946-1984

———————

Ulysses S. Dearing was born poor in Virginia, in a small hamlet in the foothills of the Blue Ridge Mountains. As a young man he moved to Pittsburgh to build a better life, but it wasn't until he moved to Cleveland that he made his mark. There, he became the first black restaurateur to own a major restaurant, and dedicated his life to serving a community many others willfully ignored.

Dearing was in Cleveland by the early 1930s, and opened a chicken take-out counter on Cedar Avenue. He used to say that the reason restaurants fail so quickly is because they try to serve too many different things. "Me, I do chicken, so I figured I'll make the best chicken I possibly can. Find out what you do well and become the best at it.'"[169]

His reputation for the best chicken started to spread, and in 1946 he opened his first restaurant, Dearing's, on East 105th Street. 105th Street was a popular thoroughfare in the neighborhood of Glenville, which at the time was transitioning from being predominantly Jewish to predominantly black. Soon after, he opened another fine-dining establishment a few blocks away. "At the time the city was segregated and he wanted his community to be able to experience what he called 'Captain-style' service," said his granddaughter Trachey McCorry.

Dearing's restaurants seemed to combine impeccable service with comfort food. McCorry remembers getting dressed up for supper, where she would order chicken giblets with gravy and rice. Dearing still focused on chicken almost every way, from fried to stewed. By 1969, he was reportedly frying 5,000 chickens and baking 500 pies a week.[170] His success led him to continue opening outposts across the city, and even the Dearing's Party Center in the Lee Harvard neighborhood, a place where his community could host wedding receptions and other social occasions.

Places like Dearing's were an important addition to the black community, as racism was still prevalent. But Dearing and other black business owners made a point of supporting each other. According to McCorry, every Monday, Dearing and other black owners of food service businesses would frequent each other's establishments, and encouraged others to support them. Experiences like that led the black community to rally around Dearing's restaurants. At one point he was reportedly making $3 million a year from them.

By the time Dearing died in 1984, there was one restaurant left on Superior Avenue, and he specified in his will that it be sold, not wanting his family to follow him into such a difficult business. It's easy to praise Ulysses Dearing for working hard and finding success in the face of so much prejudice. But it's also easy to forget that those prejudices still exist, that there are still few black-owned restaurants in Cleveland, and that no one should have to overcome such adversity. Ulysses Dearing did an extraordinary thing. Hopefully, eventually, it will be seen as ordinary.

DEARING'S CHICKEN STEW WITH CORNMEAL DUMPLINGS

Chicken and dumplings is one of the all-time American comfort foods, and Dearing's recipe is as comforting as anything. The twist is the addition of chicken livers to the dumplings, an ingredient that's not often seen anymore in recipes like these, which adds another layer of depth to the chicken.

SERVES 6-8

1 (3 to 5 lb [1.3 to 2.2 kg]) chicken

1 tbsp (15 g) salt, divided

5 chicken livers

1 tbsp (15 ml) vegetable oil

1 cup (170 g) cornmeal

⅔ cup (158 ml) chicken stock

1 tsp (5 g) parsley, chopped

1 egg, beaten

Cut up the chicken, and cover with hot water (about 6 cups [1.4 L]) and 2 teaspoons (10 g) salt. Cover and simmer for about 1½ hours, until the chicken is tender and falling off the bone.

While the chicken is simmering, sauté the chicken livers in oil over medium-high heat until cooked through and slightly browned, about 5 minutes. Let cool, then chop. Mix the cornmeal and the remaining salt in a large bowl. Add 2 tablespoons (30 ml) boiling water and stir constantly, until the mixture is just moistened. Then add the chicken stock, parsley, egg and chopped chicken livers. Refrigerate the mixture for an hour.

Bring the chicken stew to a low boil. Remove the dumpling mixture from the fridge, and drop onto the top of the stew by the heaping tablespoon (20 g) enough for about 12 dumplings. Cover and cook for another 15 minutes. Skim excess fat and serve.

[171] For reference information see Endnotes.

SAN-DAR SMORGASBORD

Bellville, Ohio
1947-1994

———·———

In 1939, a rotating smorgasbord called The Three Crowns was featured at the World's Fair in the Swedish pavilion. It was 11 feet (3.3 m) in diameter, and visitors could feast on "80 different varieties of food from this indigenous table."[172] A far cry from any traditional Scandinavian smorgasbord, where courses were eaten in a very particular order, it became the precursor to the American buffet, and it was a hit, with nearly half a million visitors. It soon became one of the most popular ways to eat across the country.

In 1947, Eugene Banks of Bellville, Ohio, double-parked his car while his pregnant wife, Dorothy, ran inside a bakery to pick up some bread and cookies. Instead, she bought the bakery, without telling her husband, and the two started Banks Soda Grill. By 1950 they added a dining room, and Dorothy, after seeing one in Florida, thought that making a smorgasbord would be a popular idea. "My dad said, no way, there's no way we'd make any money," said Darrell Banks, son of Dorothy and Eugene,[173] "but my mom persisted. My dad gave her $50 for food, and said as soon as that ran out, they were done with the smorgasbord idea." Dorothy bought all the food she could for the money, and called all their friends to come to the restaurant and test out her dishes. "She filled the restaurant the first weekend and the second weekend," said Darrell, "and by the third weekend it was dad's idea." They decided to name the reincarnated space after their kids, Sandy and Darrell, and the San-Dar Smorgasbord was born.

Bellville was a town of about 1,500 people, halfway between Columbus and Cleveland, and in the 1950s and '60s the dining scene was not all that adventurous. There were burger grills, steakhouses and soda fountains, but San-Dar Smorgasbord was one of the few places catering to different tastes, so much so that people would drive from the bigger cities just to eat there. Their menu began with traditional Americana—fried chicken, beef dip—but expanded to include dishes nobody could get for miles. Dorothy Banks experimented with smoked oysters, frog legs, white asparagus and scallops. People wrote in to the local papers in hopes of discovering their dessert recipes, made from scratch and rarely standardized, as Dorothy Banks liked to ensure her cooking stayed special. Some did incorporate frozen or canned foods to make sure things could be made in a hurry. There were 125 items on the smorgasbord at any given time, and invoking "plenty" meant keeping those plates filled. But there was never a sacrifice for quality, and San-Dar watched as other smorgasbords in the state opened and shuttered after mistakenly believing that quantity was all diners were interested in.

"During the war Dorothy worked in an airplane factory," says Darrell, "she was a heck of a hard worker, and an excellent cook. She could think out of the box and come up with really inventive ideas," which is what people remembered. Darrell has multiple stories of interactions everywhere from Germany to the Grand Tetons, of people remembering "that great restaurant" they used to go to in Bellville, before he'd pull out a postcard and say it was his. But by the late 70s, the Banks' noticed the skyrocketing gas prices were having an effect on business. Their regulars from Columbus and Cleveland were less likely to visit if they had to spend $20 on gas to get there, and as cars got smaller, so did tables."

At the same time, Americans had a changing idea of what fine dining should look like, and it ceased to involve a limitless selection of foods. What had once been a display of wealth and plenty now appeared gaudy and low-class, and the rise of all-you-can-eat buffets focused not on the quality and variety of the food available, but on how cheaply you could get it. San-Dar Smorgasbord could not survive as an upscale eatery when Americans began associating its format with thrift, and it closed in 1994.

The American smorgasbord represents a time in which America was ready to embrace plenty. The 1939 World's Fair showed Americans what an international, post-Depression life could look like, and by the late 1940s Americans both had the prosperity to buy the food they wanted, and the luxury of not being rationed. What represents that freedom of choice and bounty more than a table stacked with dozens of appetizers, with no limits on how much or little you could eat? America saw itself as a country of freedom, variety and culture, a world leader that absorbed all the best influences and presented them piled high, right next to each other. It was fun while it lasted.

SAN-DAR'S CASHEW NUT DRESSING

The sweetness of the cashews gives this traditional dressing (or stuffing) a twist, and by using both chopped and whole cashews each bite has texture. It's a perfect side dish for a large roast, especially during the holidays.

SERVES 6-8

7 cups (196 g) bread cubes, ideally a day or two old

4 cups (950 ml) chicken broth

⅛ tsp pepper

¾ tsp ground sage

¾ cup (175 ml) milk

1 egg

¼ cup (60 g) chopped cashews

¾ tsp onion flakes

¼ cup (60g) whole cashews

1 tsp (5 g) paprika

2 tbsp (30 ml) melted butter

Preheat the oven to 350°F (176°C).

Place the bread cubes in a large bowl. In a large saucepan, boil together the chicken broth, pepper and sage for approximately 10 minutes. Pour boiled broth over the bread cubes, mix slightly and cover with clean damp towel. Let sit to cool. When the mixture is cool, add the milk, egg, chopped cashews and onion flakes. Mix very thoroughly, and spread evenly in a 9 x 9-inch (22.8 x 22.8-cm) casserole dish. Sprinkle the dressing on top with the whole cashews, paprika and butter. Bake for about 30 minutes, until the top is well browned and it is moist but not wet.

[174] For reference information see Endnotes.

SAN-DAR'S DUTCH APPLE DESSERT

The Dutch apple dessert is not quite pie, not quite cobbler, but just as traditional and comforting as either, with a sugary, buttery crumble on top of a rich apple filling. The pecans are optional, but make for an earthy contrast to the sweetness of the filling.

MAKES 2 DESSERTS

8 apples

½ cup (100 g) sugar

1 tsp (5 g) cinnamon

½ tsp nutmeg

1 cup plus 3 tbsp (173 g) flour, separated

1 cup (237 ml) heavy cream

2 cups (440 g) brown sugar, separated

3 tbsp (45 g) butter

½ cup (100g) pecan halves

Preheat the oven to 375°F (190°C).

Wash, pare and slice the apples into a mixing bowl, and add sugar, cinnamon, nutmeg, 3 tablespoons (45 g) flour, heavy cream and 1 cup (220 g) brown sugar. Mix well and pour into two 10-inch (25.5-cm) round baking dishes. Mix the remaining brown sugar, butter and flour together until it's the consistency of pie dough, and sprinkle evenly over the apple filling. Garnish the desserts with the pecan halves. Bake for 10 minutes, then reduce oven temperature to 350°F (176°C) and bake for another 40 minutes, until apples are tender.

[175] For reference information see Endnotes.

India House

San Francisco, CA
1947-1995

———— • ————

San Francisco has long been a center for those seeking "exotic" cuisines. It's a place for the adventurous and the curious, and a place where many immigrants have found themselves welcome—to a point. Despite Americans' enthusiasm for the exotic, we take to it better when presented by familiar faces. India House is possibly the oldest Indian restaurant in the West, and became popular and respected in large part because its founder, David Richards Brown, was British. However, the British occupation didn't last forever, and eventually Indians were able to reclaim what was theirs.

India House was founded a month after India declared independence from Great Britain. David Richards Brown had been working at Shell Oil. According to a 1955 interview, he was making curry for his friends when they suggested he start his own restaurant. "There really wasn't a good curry place in town,"[176] so he and his wife, Patricia, opened India House in a small location on Clay Street. By 1949 they were so popular they moved into a bigger space described as a "proper colonial setting."[177]

Though tweaked to the English palate, and buttressed by dishes like deviled shrimp served in clam shells, the food was distinctly Indian. Or really, it was distinctly from one part of India. The British in India held Muslims in high regard, partially because they considered monotheistic religions more "civilized," and thus participated in more cultural exchange in Muslim areas like Punjab and Uttar Pradesh. These were regions where food was meat-heavy and rich, served with lots of bread, and the British soon developed a taste for korma, rogan josh and other Northern Indian foods. Dishes were made with the same blends of spices found in any Indian kitchen, and served with various sambals, chutneys and chapati. They were just also served with Pimm's Cups, the restaurant's most popular beverage pairing, and those who weren't fond of Indian food could always order a steak and kidney pie.[178]

India House also relied on image. Americans were only trustful of Indian cuisine when presented through a British lens,[179] so the decoration evoked part Colonial British Officer Hall and part Mughal empire. The staff was also made up almost entirely of Indian and Pakistani students dressed in turbans, part of Brown's intended scenery. Brown was so intent on keeping his staff foreign that in 1954 the restaurant was picketed for seventeen weeks after refusing to sign a contract with Bartenders Local 14, because the union wouldn't let him replace Indian employees with only other Indians. However, Brown would soon be replaced with an Indian himself.

Sarwan S. Gill immigrated to America from the Punjab region in 1958, and worked as a bus boy and waiter at India House while getting a degree at UC Berkeley. In 1968, he and two other Indian immigrants who had worked at the restaurant bought India House. By that time, America's perception of India was changing. The Beatles had discovered the sitar, more people were becoming vegetarian and in 1965, the Immigration and Naturalization Act allowed many Indians to emigrate to America easier than ever before. Americans didn't need their hands held by the British anymore, they were ready to experience Indian culture and cuisine from actual Indians, whose populations were growing by the year. The Browns had been serving Indian Food 101, and it was time to move on.

Gill and his co-owners made a point to introduce India House's customers to just how varied Indian cuisine could be. "Curries can have as many distinctive bouquets as wines," said Gill.[180] They also installed a tandoor oven, something traditionally Indian whose product—roast meat—was familiar to any American palate. However, they kept a lot of what the Browns had established, including the Pimm's Cups, and the menu remained curry heavy.

The restaurant closed in 1995. By that time, Indian restaurants were common across America, and were almost completely divorced from the imagery of British colonialism. Indians had emigrated from nearly every part of the subcontinent, and were bringing a variety of regional cuisines to the table, including more dishes featuring lentils and vegetables. However, curry and tandoori remain the stalwarts of any American Indian menu. Indian restaurants in America do not look like they do in India; they do not adhere to rules of region or season; and really, they don't have to. America is the melting pot, and Indian food in America goes by its own rules.

INDIA HOUSE'S "PIMM'S CUP MEATBALL CURRY"

This recipe was developed by Mr. and Mrs. Brown in the first iteration of India House, as an "ideal, foolproof curry dish for the amateur chef," and was served as a bar appetizer at India House. It's a perfect representation of British Indian cooking—all the spices and flavor available in India, translated into a bite-size snack perfect for tea. It's not a recipe you may find in an Indian household, but who's to say it's not as authentic? These meatballs pair well with Major Grey's chutney, rice, Chapati and a Pimm's Cup.

SERVES 6, APPROXIMATELY 36 MEATBALLS

Salt and pepper

2 lb (907 g) ground beef

1 tsp (5 g) ground coriander

1 tsp (5 g) ground ginger

¼ tsp ground cloves

¼ tsp ground cinnamon

2 tbsp (30 ml) vegetable oil

1 tbsp (15 g) butter

1 medium onion, finely chopped

2 cloves garlic, finely chopped

2 tbsp (10 g) curry powder

1 tbsp (15 ml) tomato purée

1½ to 2 cups (350 to 475 ml) beef stock

Lightly salt and pepper the beef, then mix with the coriander, ginger, cloves and cinnamon until the spices are distributed evenly throughout the meat. Form into meatballs, about 1¼ inch (3 cm) in diameter. In a heavy skillet, heat the oil and butter over medium heat, and add the onion and garlic, cooking until the onion is translucent, about 10 minutes. Turn the heat to medium high, and add the meatballs to the pan to brown on all sides, being careful not to crowd the pan (you may have to do this in batches). When browned, add all the meatballs back to the pan if you've cooked them in batches, and add the curry powder and the tomato purée. Stir gently with a wooden spoon until blended, then slowly add the beef stock and continue stirring. Cover and simmer for 15 to 20 minutes, until meatballs are just cooked through.

[181] For reference information see Endnotes.

India House's Lamb Curry

This recipe is credited to San Francisco's India House in, of all places, a 1970 anthology of recipes printed by the University of California, San Francisco Department of Obstetrics and Gynecology.[182] *There it is titled "Curry Korma," though it features no yogurt, cream or nut paste as most kormas do. This recipe comes from the India House menu after Sarwan Gill bought it, and certainly boasts a different, more complex flavor profile than it appears the Browns tended to serve. However, those distinctions are always subjective.*

Serves 8

4 lb (1.8 kg) lamb shoulder, fat removed, cut in 1-inch (2.5-cm) cubes

1½ tbsp (22.5 g) turmeric

3 cups (709 ml) of vegetable oil

6 medium onions, chopped

3 cloves garlic, chopped

6 whole green cardamom pods

6 bay leaves

6 whole cloves

1 cinnamon stick

¼ tsp mace

¼ tsp ginger powder

2 tbsp (30 g) ground cumin

1 tsp (5 g) ground coriander

¼ tsp red pepper

½ tsp (2.5 g) nutmeg

1½ tsp (7.5 g) dill

Salt to taste

Pat the lamb cubes dry and roll in turmeric. Heat the oil in a large saucepan over medium-high heat and add the onions and garlic. Fry, stirring occasionally, until the mixture is light brown, about 20 minutes. In a separate pot, boil the cardamom, bay leaves, cloves and cinnamon stick in 1 cup (236 ml) water for 10 minutes. In a small bowl, combine the mace, ginger powder, cumin, coriander, red pepper, nutmeg and dill and mix well. When the onions are browned, add the mace mix and cook for 10 minutes. Add the meat and salt to taste. Strain the spices that have been boiled and add the seasoned liquid to the meat. Lower the heat to medium and cook, covered, until the meat is tender, about 15 minutes. Turn off the heat and let stand for at least an hour to let the flavors meld. Reheat before serving.

RUBY CHOW'S

Seattle, WA
1948-1979

————·————

"The is one of the few restaurants in the country that refused to indulge the American palate with such artificial Chinese food as chop suey," wrote *The Ford Treasury of Famous Recipes from Famous Eating Places* in 1955. Even then, it seems, Americans were self-conscious about the authenticity of their eating habits and claimed to want a "real" experience. However, there was a mutual distrust between the Chinese and white communities—the white population shied away from Chinatown unless it was for a drunken, late-night bowl of chop suey, and in return the Chinese doubted their desire for authenticity. Ruby Chow's, Seattle's first Chinese restaurant outside of Chinatown, helped change everyone's expectations.

Historically, Seattle's Chinese restaurants had operated in Chinatown, partially due to segregation practices that made it difficult for Chinese to find jobs, homes or common services outside of that neighborhood. However, increased activism against these redlining and "racial restrictive covenant"[184] practices meant that by the late 1940s, Ruby and Ping Chow had an opportunity to open their own restaurant outside of Chinatown. They bought an old mansion in the Capitol Hill neighborhood, transforming it into a Chinese restaurant, and moving the whole family into the rooms upstairs. Ping Chow assumed the duties of chef, cooking more traditional Cantonese cuisine than the "chop suey joints" would provide.

The more traditional food was a hit with the non-Chinese, including celebrities and politicians, likely because it was presented with the familiarity of a fine-dining setting. This was a calculated move on Ruby Chow's part, who intended the restaurant to not be just a restaurant, but a cultural introduction to the beauty and importance of Chinese culture. By serving Chinese food on white tablecloths with impeccable service, the food no longer came with the class and racial connotations of eating at a restaurant in Chinatown. At the restaurant's peak, they could seat 300 for a banquet dinner, serving dishes like Beggar's Chicken, pressed duck and melon soup. The city's Chinese dined there too, enjoying the traditional cuisine and watching non-Chinese enjoy it as well.

Ruby Chow was a popular hostess, and was known as the matriarch of Seattle's Chinese community.[186] She co-founded the Chinese Community Girls Drill Team, and she and Ping sponsored other community activities, especially for young Chinese women who had few opportunities. Chow later became the first female president of the Chong Wah Benevolent Association, and later, the first Asian-American woman to serve as a King County councilwoman, where she would continue her mission to improve the knowledge and image of the Chinese community. To balance that new work, the restaurant had to give. In 1979 they leased the restaurant to another family,[187] and by 1980 it was bankrupt.[188] But its 31-year run had an incredible impact on Seattle, helping to bridge gaps between the Chinese and non-Chinese populations. Chow inspired other Chinese to open restaurants outside of Chinatown, and paved the way for non-Chinese to be receptive of the culture. And she proved to both sides that a Chinese-American woman was capable of being a host, a leader and an inspiration.

Ruby Chow's Melon Soup

This light soup is an example of the kind of Chinese-American cooking customers would not have found in other "chop suey joints." As the soup is served, the poached egg breaks up, releasing the yolk into the soup and thickening it, while the water chestnuts add a good crunch.

SERVES 4

1 qt (946 ml) chicken stock

¼ lb (113 g) raw pork, diced

3 water chestnuts, peeled and sliced

Salt to taste

1 lb (453 g) winter melon, cut into 1-inch (2.5-cm) pieces

4 eggs

Pour the stock into a 2 quart (1.9 L) saucepan and bring to a rapid boil. Add the pork and sliced water chestnuts, and boil, covered, until the pork is almost cooked through, about 15 to 20 minutes. Add the salt and melon, and boil for another 10 minutes, uncovered. Break the eggs into each serving bowl then pour the hot soup evenly over the raw eggs, being sure the eggs remain whole. Serve immediately.

[189] For reference information see Endnotes.

PAOLI'S RESTAURANT

San Francisco, CA

1951-1984

In Frank Capra's *It's A Wonderful Life*, Mr. Potter refers to an Italian community as a bunch of "garlic eaters." It's hard to imagine an America in which that would be an insult, but at the time Italian food was still highly unwelcome in refined, white society. It was immigrant food, "ethnic" and Mr. Potter's prejudices would have been shared by many when the film was released in 1946. However, Capra, as an Italian immigrant, perhaps knew change was around the corner, and that Mr. Potter's views would be challenged in due time.

In 1951, Joe and Rita Paoli opened Paoli's Restaurant in San Francisco, taking over the old bar and chophouse Collins & Wheeland. It was a time when San Franciscans were ready to dine on something a little more worldly than the steaks and oysters available at every bar that had existed since the Gold Rush. The war was over, after all, and America was now a key player in global politics—we might as well eat like it. Paoli's served Italian cuisine, but with more of a mind to continental and Californian tastes than to Old Country authenticity. It was not an East Coast red sauce joint. Ravioli appetizers were deep fried, baked cannelloni was made with chicken, and both were offered alongside Steak Béarnaise and French Pancakes Balzac, served on crisp linen tablecloths by tuxedoed waiters.

Joe Paoli's parents immigrated to America from Camaiore, Italy, and moved to San Francisco, where there was already a sizable Northern Italian population, when Joe was a child. From a young age he worked in restaurants around the city, and maintained creative control in Paoli's kitchen. "We'd go to other restaurants and taste something we liked, and he'd go back and try to make it again," said Rita Paoli,[190] who said he was also inspired by her mother's Italian cooking. But it was the atmosphere that kept people filing in for happy hour, munching on fried calamari and lasagna with their cocktails. Rita Paoli scoured the city searching for decor to match the old Victorian building, and as they expanded, each new room got a theme—the Lordship room, the Pinafore, the Dead-Eye Dick room. It was an aesthetic common to the era in California. "All these restaurants were from the beginning highly themed places, self-consciously aware that they were offering a stylized and theatrical performance alongside food and drink," wrote Kevin Starr in *Golden Dreams: California in an Age of Abundance*.[191] How theatrical? Rita Paoli remembered the Josephine's Pearl cocktail, which was garnished with a gardenia petal and cultured pearl. "In those days we bought the pearls by the bag."

Paoli's was at the center of San Francisco's fine-dining scene, to the point where, when Greece's royalty came to visit, Mayor George Christopher called to reserve the Lordship room for them. And Joe Paoli was so well known that, when a visiting prince asked where to find a car so he could drive out to the country, he handed over the keys to his new Cadillac convertible, saying to "leave it on any street corner with a note that it belongs to me, and it'll find its way back." However, that high proved short lived. By the 1960s, American's were increasingly disinterested in "dining" as an event, especially if it meant wearing a jacket and tie, as Paoli's and many others required. In 1969 they closed and changed locations to make way for the Bank of America towers, but the new location never caught on as much. "We closed in 1984, it was just time. Our era was gone. We saw the beginning of an era after the war was over, and we saw the end of it," said Rita Paoli.

Diners are less willing to pay for atmosphere now, unless it's accompanied by "authenticity," and Italian food has ceased to be a new novelty. It has woven itself into American cuisine, not just in flavor, but in style. Paoli's was one of a new crop of restaurants that built on traditions "established by the provincial Italian restauranteurs of serving an abundance of food in a congenial atmosphere that made diners feel they were dining, and not just eating," wrote Deanna Paoli Gumina, Joe and Rita's daughter.[192] This is now the expectation of what a restaurant should be. Places like Paoli's just did it first.

PAOLI'S BAKED CANNELLONI

This recipe was given to me by Rita Paoli, who said it was one of their most beloved dishes. The stuffing is made with veal and chicken "roasted until the meat fell off the bone, and then hand chopped," so this is a great recipe for leftovers if you've made a veal or chicken roast. The restaurant also used fresh crêpes for the cannelloni, though fresh sheets of pasta from a local specialty store can be substituted. The result is an extravagant and flavorful dish, with lighter and fresher flavors than you may have come to expect from your average baked cannelloni.

SERVES 4

FOR THE CRÊPES

3 eggs

2 tbsp (30 g) all-purpose flour

1 tsp (5 ml) water

1 tbsp (15 ml) milk

Pinch of salt

1 tbsp (15 ml) olive oil

FOR THE SAUCE

1 (28-oz [790-g]) can whole, peeled San Marzano tomatoes

3 tbsp (45 ml) olive oil

½ yellow onion, finely chopped

1 garlic clove, finely chopped

FOR THE FILLING

½ lb (225 g) veal stew meat

3 chicken thighs

1 garlic clove, finely chopped

1 shallot, minced

1 sprig fresh thyme

4–5 fresh sage leaves

¼ tsp freshly grated nutmeg

Salt and pepper to taste

15 oz (425 g) ricotta cheese

1 egg

⅓ cup (60 g) Parmesan cheese, shredded

To make the crêpes, whisk 3 eggs, the flour, water, milk and a pinch of salt in a bowl. Cover and refrigerate for at least 3 hours, or up to overnight. Heat the olive oil in a small saucepan or crêpe pan over medium heat, and add about 3 tablespoons (45 g) of batter to create a round crêpe 5 inches (12.5 cm) in diameter. Cook until edges are firm, about 3 minutes, then flip and cook until edges just curl, another 3 minutes. This should make approximately eight crêpes.

To make the sauce, purée the tomatoes. Heat the olive oil over medium heat, then add the onion and garlic and cook until the onion is translucent, about 10 minutes. Add the tomato purée to the pan and simmer, uncovered, until thickened, about half an hour.

Preheat the oven to 350°F (176°C). To make the filling, in a small roasting pan, combine the veal and chicken with the garlic, shallot, thyme, sage, nutmeg, salt and pepper. Roast for about half an hour, until meat is cooked through. Discard the thyme sprigs and let cool. Finely chop the meat (either by hand or in a food processor), and combine with the roasted shallot seasonings, ricotta and one egg.

Raise the oven heat to 400°F (204°C). Spread a few spoonfuls of the tomato sauce over the bottom of a 9 x 9-inch (22.8 x 22.8-cm) casserole dish. Spoon the filling into the crêpes, then roll into tubes and place seam-side down in the dish. Cover the cannelloni with sauce, and sprinkle with Parmesan cheese. Cook until cheese and sauce bubbles, about 20 minutes.

[193] For reference information see Endnotes.

Paoli's Pickled Celery with Anchovies

The bar at Paoli's was all about finger foods, like these lemony, herbal pickles served with anchovies, for some real 1960s flavor. These work well as an appetizer, but also as a side at the dinner table.

Serves 4

4 celery hearts

Water to cover

Juice of 6½ lemons

1 pt (½ L) vegetable oil

½ pt (¼ L) white wine vinegar

1 clove of garlic, crushed

1 tbsp (15 g) parsley, chopped

1 tsp (5 g) oregano

Dash of cayenne pepper

1 sprig thyme

1 bay leaf

Salt and pepper to taste

1 (2-oz [55-g]) tin of flat anchovy filets

½ medium pimiento, sliced

Trim, wash and halve four young celery hearts of equal size. Cover with water and juice of half a lemon, and boil for about 8 minutes, until it starts to soften. Meanwhile, mix the remaining lemon juice, oil, vinegar, garlic, parsley, oregano, cayenne, thyme, bay leaf, salt and pepper in a small saucepan and bring to a boil. Add the celery to the liquid and cook until it's tender, about another 5 minutes. Let cool, then put the celery and marinade in an airtight container and store in the refrigerator until completely cold. When ready to serve, remove the celery to a serving plate and garnish with anchovies and pimiento, and a few drops of the cooking liquor.

[194] For reference information see Endnotes.

WOLFIE'S RASCAL HOUSE

Miami, FL
1954-2008

———·———

In 1950, 55,000 Jews lived in Miami. By 1970, 80 percent of the population of Miami Beach was Jewish. They came for the reasons anyone came: tourism, the booming real estate industry, warmth. That's why Wilfred "Wolfie" Cohen came in the early 1940s too, and he'd eventually become the name behind some of Miami Beach's most iconic Jewish-style restaurants.

Cohen was born in Schenectady, New York, the son of German-Americans who owned a jewelry store. At a young age he dropped out of school to work as a busboy in the Jewish resorts of the Catskills. "There were a lot of entertainers there," said his daughter, Robin Sherwood. "They all knew him, and eventually they'd come down to his restaurants in Miami."[195] During World War II the army wouldn't take him because of his bad back, so he and a friend from Brooklyn moved to Miami. He quickly found work mixing salads in hotels, and eventually decided to buy an eight-seat deli called Al's Sandwich Shop, which he soon sold to open Wolfie's Deli. Cohen was not yet 30.

"It was a destination," says Sherwood. "People would get up and go to Wolfie's, go out and run errands and come back for lunch. They were the rascals. They'd come for three meals a day." It was also the beginning of a trend of Cohen buying and selling his delis. After a few years Cohen sold Wolfie's, which would continue to operate successfully until 2002, and opened Pumpernick's, and in 1954, Wolfie's Rascal House. The Rascal House was a combination of refined dining spot and New York deli, where you could get corned beef at the counter or a steak dinner made from their house-aged beef. Wolfie's Rascal House caught Miami Beach's Jewish population on the rise. The three-meal-a-day "rascals" were probably there so often given the prevalence of kitchen-less boarding rooms on the beach, and because of the familiar cuisine. However, the broadness of the menu attracted just about everybody. If whitefish and pickles weren't always a part of Miami's culinary repertoire, they became so now. Lines out the door were a frequent sight, and there were always celebrity visitors.

Cohen was a character. He purposely wore clothes that didn't match to make people "sit up and pay attention," and could usually be seen working the floor, making sure everything was in order. He was also notoriously picky about his food. According to Sherwood, to ensure they got the best quality eggs, Cohen bought his own chicken farm. To get the best quality cloth napkins, he put someone in business to make just those. "We can afford to do what others can't," stated the menu, which showed an overhead diagram of the kitchen, bake shop and work rooms. The size of the Rascal House, they argued, gave them purchasing power, allowing them to serve with "better quality, larger portions and reasonable prices."

The Rascal House continued after the population began to change. The boarding houses were replaced by upscale hotels, the Jewish population moved north or left altogether, "and the younger newcomers—often from South America and Europe—have proved far less interested in items like pastrami or potato pancakes," wrote the *New York Times* on the occasion of its closing.[196] Tastes had changed, but likely, so had the realities of running a business that large. Nowadays when we think of quality, we think small. It's small-batch ingredients and boutique restaurants, an experience you share with a select few. It's not 5,000 covers a night, and while large-scale delis like this still exist, it's hard to imagine one could open today. The Rascal House was a product, and then a victim, of both the demands and the logistics of its time.

WOLFIE'S SOUR CREAM STREUSEL CAKE

The streusel cake served at Wolfie's Rascal House came from Wolfie Cohen's wife, Miriam Rose, and was scaled up to serve hundreds of hungry customers. Eventually they added apples to the cake, but the original recipe here, a crumbly layered coffee cake, needs no dressing up. Serve it warm with strong coffee.

SERVES 6 TO 8

2½ cups (320 g) all-purpose flour

2 tsp (10 g) baking powder

A pinch of salt

½ cup (113 g) butter

1 cup (201 g) sugar

1 cup (236 ml) sour cream

2 tbsp (30 ml) milk

3 eggs

1 tsp (5 ml) vanilla

STREUSEL

1 cup (240 g) pecans, finely chopped

½ cup (100 g) sugar

1 tsp (5 g) cinnamon

Preheat the oven to 350°F (176°C).

In a large bowl, sift together the flour, baking powder and salt. In a mixer, cream together the butter and sugar. Slowly add the sour cream and milk to the butter and mix until combined. Add the eggs one at a time, waiting until each is fully incorporated into the batter. Then, add the flour mixture, a little at a time until incorporated. Add the vanilla and mix on high speed for 2 to 3 minutes, until completely smooth. In a separate bowl, combine all the ingredients for the streusel.

Pour half of the batter into a greased, 10-inch (25.4-cm) tube pan. Sprinkle half of the streusel over the batter, then cover with the remaining batter, and top with the remaining streusel. Bake for about an hour, until a tester inserted in the cake comes out clean.

[197] For reference information see Endnotes.

WOLFIE'S CHEESECAKE

"A beautiful rich, moist cake" is how Wolfie's cheesecake was described in 1959. It's so moist probably because there's no flour (and oddly, no crust), just cream cheese, eggs and enough sugar and cornstarch to hold it together. The result is an almost custard-like slice, neither overly sweet nor thick. It does well with a garnish of fresh fruit.

SERVES 8

1½ lb (780 g) cream cheese

Scant ¾ cup (5 oz) sugar

3 tbsp and ½ tsp (47.5 g) cornstarch

3 eggs

Preheat the oven to 450°F (232°C).

Using the paddle attachment on a mixer, soften the cream cheese. Add sugar and cornstarch and blend until smooth. Add the eggs one at a time until they're fully incorporated.

Pour into a greased, circular baking pan resting in a large pan filled with water. Bake until brown on top, about 35 minutes. Lower the oven to 350°F (176°C) and bake until a cake tester comes out clean, about 10 minutes.

[198] For reference information see Endnotes.

WOLFIE'S CHOCOLATE BROWNIES

The recipe for these decadent, fudgy chocolate brownies came from Florence Cohen, Wolfie's mother, and according to Robin Sherwood, they were well-known and loved by many Wolfie's regulars. The brownies would be displayed in a pyramid on top of the counter at Wolfie's Rascal House, tempting diners as they were led to their seats.

MAKES 9 BROWNIES

1 cup (128 g) flour

Pinch of salt

2 cups (480 g) chopped walnuts

4 oz (113 g) unsweetened baking chocolate

1 cup (227 g) unsalted butter

4 eggs

2 cups (402 g) sugar

2 tsp (10 ml) vanilla extract

Powdered sugar for garnish

Preheat the oven to 350°F (176°C).

Whisk together the flour, salt and nuts, and set aside. Melt the chocolate and butter over a double boiler, then remove from heat and let cool about 6 minutes. Beat together the eggs and sugar, then add them into the chocolate sauce. Add the vanilla. Gently fold the flour mixture into the chocolate, until almost incorporated. The flour should still be visible in the batter and not completely blended in.

Pour the batter evenly into a greased 8 x 8-inch (20.3 x 20.3-cm) square pan, and bake for 20 to 25 minutes. They should still be creamy and soft when removed from the oven, and will dry as they cool. Let cool completely, and dust with powdered sugar.

WOLFIE'S ROAST CHICKEN WITH CHALLAH STUFFING

Another recipe from the Cohen family's personal collection that made it onto the menu, this time from Wolfie Cohen's mother-in-law, Renee Goldhaber, this simple chicken with stuffing got a Jewish deli twist with the use of challah. The challah makes for a flavorful, moist stuffing that absorbs the flavor of the chicken without drying it out.

SERVES 6

1 loaf challah, approximately 1 lb (435 g)

3 tbsp (45 g) butter, separated

1 large onion, chopped

2 stalks celery, chopped

3 cups (709 ml) water

3 eggs

Paprika, salt, pepper and garlic powder to taste

1 (5 lb [2.2 kg]) roasting chicken

Heat the oven to 350°F (176°C). Chop the challah into 1-inch (2.5-cm) cubes and lay on a baking sheet. Dry in the oven for about 10 minutes, then let cool.

Heat 2 tablespoons (30 g) of the butter in a saucepan. Sauté the chopped onion and celery until they are translucent, about 10 minutes, and set aside to cool. Soak the challah briefly in 3 cups (709 ml) water for 1 minute, then gently squeeze out the water and place the bread in a large mixing bowl. Save the water in the bowl for basting if more liquid is needed while roasting. Mix in the cooked onion and celery, and gently mix in the eggs. Season the stuffing with paprika, garlic powder, salt and pepper to taste.

Wash the chicken and pat dry. Rub the remaining butter all over the skin, and season with salt, garlic powder and paprika inside and outside, so that it's well colored and you can see a good salt crust. Dress the chicken using the stuffing inside the cavity.

Heat the oven to 450°F (232°C). Place the chicken in a roaster, covered, and roast for 10 minutes. Then reduce the temperature to 350°F (176°C) and roast for 20 minutes per pound (450 g). Uncover the chicken for the last 10 minutes to brown. Remove when a meat thermometer inserted into the inner thigh reads 165°F (74°C). The skin should be dark and crisp.

Roast the remaining stuffing in a baking dish alongside the chicken for 40 minutes.

KAHIKI SUPPER CLUB

Columbus, OH
1961-2000

The first thought that crosses one's mind when looking at the Kahiki Supper Club is, "What on earth is this doing in Columbus, Ohio?" But in 1961 Tiki culture was alive and thriving, thanks to hoards of men who had returned from the Pacific Theater with a taste for exotic fruit juices and vaguely Polynesian aesthetics. Places like Don the Beachcomber and Trader Vic's on the West Coast spearheaded the culinary movement in the 1930s, but post-WW II there were just that many more people with a misguided nostalgia for the South Pacific, whose cravings could be satisfied with plastic leis and drinks served out of novelty mugs. Hawaii's new statehood in 1959 only added fuel to the fire.

Lee Henry and Bill Sapp, steakhouse owners in Columbus, decided that Ohio's capital needed it's own Tiki parlor. They traveled to the West Coast for inspiration, and went with their designer to the newly opened Mai Kai in Ft. Lauderdale, Florida. "Posing as tourists—they took snapshots and pocketed menus," according to *Imbibe* magazine,[199] and returned to Ohio to open a bar, the Grass Shack. When that burned down, they created what became one of the most ostentatious Tiki restaurants in the country. They spent a million dollars on the 500-seat restaurant, at a time when the capital still had fewer than half a million people. The building was supposedly inspired by men's meeting houses in New Guinea, and featured two Easter Island statues, heads aflame, directing customers to a bamboo bridge. Never mind that these were all independent, robust cultures that were being mashed together and distorted for the pleasures of middle-class Americans.

The food was entirely invented, masquerading as traditional, and has now become traditional on its own terms. There were egg rolls and crab rangoon and orange-glazed duck. There were multiple things one could order that came served in a pineapple. The drinks were topped with umbrellas and flowers and fire. The "mystery drink" served four and was delivered to the table by a beautiful woman as gongs sounded. According to a pamphlet from the restaurant, "Most of the cocktail waitresses are the wives of servicemen or ex-servicemen and all are from Japan or Korea."[200] And for a while, it was the place to go in Columbus, as much theme park as restaurant. It became a legendary spot for Tiki enthusiasts, who exclaimed things like "a part of me died"[201] when it closed in 2000. Locals rallied to save it, arguing that its 1997 inclusion on the National Register of Historic Places should count for something, but to no avail. It was torn down and replaced by a Walgreens.[202]

The Kahiki, as with every other Tiki restaurant, started out by using the South Pacific and its cultures as a prop, an homage that faltered into a caricature. The cultures and traditions of many Pacific Islanders were distilled into a "theme" (for instance, "Tiki" is an important figure in Maori mythology). However, American Tiki culture has morphed into a tradition all its own, like American Chinese food or deep-dish pizza. Coming to it now, few would mistake crab rangoon or zombies as authentic Pacific Island cuisine, and influence has begun to go both ways—a friend living in Tahiti recently sent me a photo of her sipping on a mai tai.

Many of our culinary traditions have problematic origins, and it is often difficult to tell appropriation from cultural exchange. It serves us well to remember these histories. Tiki has never accurately represented the cultures of the Pacific Islands. Instead, it represents the aspirations of Americans, done with a war, ready to travel, and letting themselves fantasize with a sweet pineapple drink and "exotic" waitresses in bikinis in the middle of Ohio. It is a parody that has become as real as the things it parodied. Places like the Kahiki represent nothing but themselves, but that history is fascinating in its own right.

KAHIKI'S POLYNESIAN SPELL PUNCH

One of the appeals of Tiki bars is the complexity of the cocktails, since the average home bar usually doesn't boast such varied ingredients. The Kahiki's Polynesian Spell was served as a single cocktail, but for home consumption (and to justify the numerous ingredients) it works especially well as a punch. Be warned, it makes for a strong drink, but that's the whole point of Tiki, isn't it?

SERVES 8-10

10 tsp (50 g) sugar

Juice of 10 lemons

20 oz (530 ml) grape juice

30 oz (800 ml) dry gin

5 oz (130 ml) triple sec

5 oz (130 ml) peach brandy

Extra lemon slices for garnish

Dissolve the sugar in the lemon juice. Combine ingredients (except the lemons) in a punch bowl over an ice ring, and mix well. Garnish with lemon slices, and serve ladled into punch cups.

[203] For reference information see Endnotes.

KAHIKI'S TAHITIAN MERMAID

This recipe was provided to the Ohio Department of Agriculture by Mickey Cheung, former chef of the Kahiki.
Crab- and cream-cheese-stuffed steak is a prime example of the opulence found at the Kahiki,
recipes that hint at a tropical origin but feature distinctly American ingredients.

SERVES 2

FILLING

3½ oz (100 g) crabmeat

3½ oz (100 g) cream cheese

½ cup (120 g) bread crumbs

¼ tsp hot sauce

¼ tsp Worcestershire sauce

Salt and pepper to taste

⅛ tsp garlic powder

Juice of ½ a lemon

1 tbsp (15 g) chopped onion

2 (6 oz [170 g]) beef filets

½ tsp Worcestershire sauce

½ tsp seasoning salt

¼ tsp pepper

2 tbsp (30 ml) vegetable oil

Combine all the filling ingredients in a bowl and set aside.

Butterfly the filets of beef so they are still attached on one side. Season the insides with the Worcestershire sauce, salt and pepper.

Heat the oil in a large skillet over high heat. Pan-fry the inner part of the steaks over high heat for 30 seconds. Remove the steaks from the pan, and stuff half of the filling into each steak and slightly close it. Pan-fry each of the outer sides of the steaks on high heat for 1 minute, and serve.

[204] For reference information see Endnotes.

Chicken Pineapple Kahiki

This recipe was originally published in 1969, allegedly from the Kahiki's executive chef. The tart and sweet pineapple-chicken stir-fry is served in hollowed-out pineapple shells. It's a fusion of flavors that could only exist in the Tiki world, and a kitschy presentation to match.

SERVES 2

1 pineapple

2 chicken breasts, cut into ½-inch (1.25-cm) pieces

1 tbsp (15 ml) white wine

1½ cups (354 ml) water, separated

1 green bell pepper, diced

½ cup (120 g) sugar

½ cup (118 ml) vinegar

½ cup (118 ml) ketchup

Pinch of ground ginger

Pinch of garlic powder

1 tsp (5 g) cornstarch

Cut the pineapple in half lengthwise. Scoop out the fruit from the shell, leaving a ½ inch (1.25 cm) of pineapple in the shell. Discard the pineapple core, and dice the scooped-out pineapple into ½-inch (1.25-cm) pieces.

Heat a large skillet over medium heat. Add the chicken and wine and cook until the chicken is browned. Add a cup (236 ml) of water, the diced pineapple and green pepper to the skillet. Mix the remaining water with the sugar, vinegar, ketchup, ginger and garlic powder. Add the mixture to the skillet, and stir until combined. Place the 2 pineapple halves cut-side down over the chicken mixture. Cook until the chicken is cooked through, about 5 minutes. Transfer the pineapple shells to plates.

Mix the cornstarch with a little water and add to skillet. Cook until the juices are thickened, another few minutes, then serve the chicken in the pineapple shells.

[205] For reference information see Endnotes.

MAXIM'S CHICAGO

Chicago, IL
1963-1982

———

You may already know about Maxim's Paris, the art nouveau monolith that became a the place to be seen for artists, writers and the generally rich from the early 1900s through the 1970s. Now, it has become an amber-sealed symbol for all things belle-epoque, and certainly earned its nickname of the "world's most famous restaurant."

But there was also Maxim's Chicago.

In 1963, Maxim's in Chicago opened as a franchise of its Parisian counterpart by architect Bertrand Goldberg and his wife Nancy. According to their son, Geoff,[206] Bertrand Goldberg had decided his Astor Towers would be a hotel, and that the hotel needed a restaurant. "He went to my grandmother, Lillian Florsheim, an artist who grew up with money and understood elegance, and he asks 'What's the best restaurant in the world?' My father was impetuous in this way, and she said, 'Maxim's in Paris.' So he set up this whole French cultural show in the hotel, and talked the owner of Maxim's into setting up a franchise." It was a nearly exact replica, down to the red banquettes and the Mucha-designed china, products of Goldberg's exacting creativity. And while Paris had no issues being known as a center of fine cuisine, Maxim's helped put Chicago on the map.

Nancy Goldberg wound up running the restaurant by accident. "Paris was supposed to send over managers but they don't work out, and all of a sudden they're about to open and no one is in charge, and she just jumps in," said Geoff. She began interviewing chefs and learning about food. And her taste shaped what would eventually be the Ur-restaurant for Chicago's fine dining scene. "Chicago was a meat-and-potatoes town, and basically, they brought culture in." Maxim's served haute French cuisine, the type made with impeccable skill, just as Americans were learning the pleasures French food could bring (*Mastering the Art of French Cooking* was published in 1961). "Very quickly," wrote the *Chicago Tribune*, "those who rated restaurants in the city and the world began praising Maxim's and sprinkling stars on it."[207]

Geoff remembers just the type of lengths his mother was willing to go to ensure a special, elegant experience at Maxim's. "My sister and I went to France in the '70s, and my mom said we had to go to Corsica to get this pâté they made from thrushes. We buy maybe 20 cases of it, and have to ship it to all of her friends from Marseilles. They were ecstatic, thinking it was for them and my mother had to remind them it was for the restaurant, and went around picking it all up."

The grand dining rooms of places like Maxim's fell out of favor with "a belt-tightening economy and a new breed of diners," who had grown tired of the traditional and the formal. The '80s, after all, were the dawn of "fusion," both in cuisine and in dining experience, where expensive cuisine didn't have to come with a waiter in black tie. Goldberg perhaps understood the trends, and decided to close Maxim's after 19 years, preferring to shutter instead of catering to different tastes. But even after that short time, its impact was felt. Many of the chefs Nancy Goldberg coaxed from France went on to open their own fine-dining establishments across the city, like Le Bordeaux, Kiki's Bistro and Le Vichyssois. Chicago is now a center of American experimental cuisine, as cosmopolitan as the coasts. Yet somehow, never going so far as to insult its meat-and-potatoes heritage.

Bertrand Goldberg designed iconic buildings like Marina City and St. Joseph's hospital. He said of his own works, "I am talking about the performance of people in a social system, about the performance of people in the city."[208] His buildings were fluid forms, curving, cartoonish feats of concrete that managed to be entirely reasonable. They were apartment buildings, hospitals and schools, never so removed from their surroundings that they forgot to serve the people they were built to inhabit. It is no surprise that he would be attracted to a place like Maxim's, not just for the arc of its art nouveau design, but because it relied on perfection that was at once ornate and practical. It was a waiter in a tuxedo serving you a classic butter-poached sole. It was models in Givenchy dresses lounging in red banquettes, eating Corsican thrush pâté. It made sense, but you could never mistake it for being ordinary.

Maxim's Flan de Carrotes

Rather than a typical flan, this dish consists of a thick, savory, carrot-flavored custard baked into a short pastry crust. It's an elegant, rich way to serve carrots, and emblematic of the opulence of a place like Maxim's.

Serves 8

SHORT PASTRY CRUST

2 cups (256 g) flour

12 tbsp (170 g) softened butter

¼ tsp salt

2 tbsp (30 g) sugar (optional)

½ cup (118 ml) cold water

1¾ lb (793 g) carrots

½ cup water

Pinch of salt

½ cup (100 g) sugar

1 cup (227 g) butter

½ cup (118 ml) cream

Salt and pepper to taste

To make the pastry crust, pour the flour into a mixing bowl. Place the butter, salt and sugar, if using, in the center and knead together quickly. Add the cold water and knead together delicately and rapidly, making a dough that is homogenous but not elastic (the result of too much kneading). Roll into a ball, wrap in waxed paper and refrigerate for at least 2 hours. If possible, chill overnight.

Preheat the oven to 425°F (218°C). Line a 9-inch (23-cm) buttered pie pan with the chilled pastry dough. Press down firmly, trim the edges and prick in several places with a fork to avoid bubbles. Line with wax paper and spread with dried beans or pie weights. Bake until the crust is a light golden color, about 15 minutes. Remove paper and weights, and return to oven for another 5 minutes. Remove the crust from the oven and set aside.

Peel and wash the carrots and cut them in thin slices. Cook ½ cup (120 g) of carrots in boiling salted water until tender, and set aside. Stew the remaining slices in a ½ cup (118 ml) water with a pinch of salt, pinch of sugar and ½ cup (113 g) butter. When tender, the juice should be nearly reduced. Purée the stewed carrots and add the remaining butter, bit by bit. Add the cream, mix thoroughly, reheat in a small saucepan and pour into the pastry shell. Decorate with slices of boiled carrots, sprinkle with the remaining sugar, and bake for 20 minutes.

[209] For reference information see Endnotes.

MAXIM'S SOLES ALBERT

Maxim's Chicago served many of the same dishes as its Parisian counterpart, including this popular butter-poached sole, seasoned lightly with vermouth and fresh herbs. If sole is unavailable, flounder makes a good substitute.

SERVES 3

3 (1 lb [453 g]) sole

1 lb (453 g) butter

3 shallots, chopped

½ tbsp (7 g) chopped parsley

½ tbsp (7 g) tarragon

¾ cup (180 g) fresh bread crumbs

Salt and pepper to taste

1½ cups (354 ml) dry vermouth

½ lemon

Remove the heads, tails, fins and skin from both sides of the sole and clean them. With a very sharp pointed knife make an incision along the dorsal bone.

Melt ¾ cup (180 g) of butter in a casserole dish large enough to fit the three sole side by side. Mix together the shallots, parsley and tarragon, and spread the mixture in the bottom of the dish.

Preheat the oven to 425°F (218°C). Melt ½ cup (120 g) butter in another pan. Dip the side of the fish formerly covered in white skin in this butter, then in the bread crumbs. Place the fish breaded side up in the casserole dish. Season with salt and pepper. Pour in enough dry vermouth to half-submerge the fish without wetting the bread crumbs. Pour another ¾ cup (180 g) melted butter over the soles. Place in the oven and brown for about 30 minutes.

Remove from the oven and place on a hot serving dish. Pour the juice in the pan into a large skillet over high heat, and reduce to almost 2 tbsp (30 ml). Remove from heat and stir in remaining butter, whisking vigorously, to obtain a light, frothy sauce. Add a squeeze of lemon; check the seasoning. Pour some of the sauce around the fish and serve the rest on the side.

[210] For reference information see Endnotes.

Maxim's Entrecotes Bercy

A broiled sirloin steak is always good on its own, but this meaty compound butter makes it even better. The beef marrow can be specially requested at most butchers, and be sure to use fresh parsley so the flavor cuts through the fat.

Serves 4

BERCY BUTTER

1½ cups (330 g) beef marrow

3 shallots, minced

1 cup (237 ml) dry white wine

1 cup (230 g) butter

1 tbsp (15 g) chopped parsley

3 tbsp (45 ml) lemon juice

Salt and pepper

3 (1 lb [453 g]) sirloin steaks

1 tbsp (15 ml) oil

Salt and pepper

8 sprigs watercress for garnish

To prepare the Bercy Butter, poach the beef marrow in simmering water for about 8 minutes. Drain, let cool and cut into tiny cubes. In a small saucepan, cook the shallots and wine over low heat, until the liquid is reduced by half. Cool, then reheat and add the softened butter, marrow, parsley, lemon juice, salt and pepper. Mix well and keep hot.

Heat the broiler to high. Brush the steaks with oil and salt and pepper to taste. Set the steaks in a broiler pan or large cast-iron skillet (big enough that they don't overlap). Broil for about 5 minutes per side for medium rare (a thermometer set in the middle of the steak should read 145°F [62°C]).

Place the steaks on a hot serving dish and garnish with watercress. Serve the Bercy Butter either on the side or spread on the steaks just before serving.

[211] For reference information see Endnotes.

M&G Diner

New York, NY
1968-2008

———·———

M&G's sign was a landmark of 125th Street. "Southern Fried Chicken," it read, "old fashion' but good," as if the two were mutually exclusive. By all accounts the fried chicken, as well as everything else they served, were both, as if you walked into a Southern kitchen in the middle of Harlem. "There was nothing like it," said Pearl Hamilton, a former cook and waitress at M&G.[212]

M&G diner was founded by Fred Gadsden and another partner, whose last name began with M, in 1968.[213] Gadsden was originally from South Carolina, and brought his wife and sister, Betty Moore, to do most of the cooking. It was an evocative year for Harlem. On one hand, it was a peak of civil rights unrest. Harlem was the scene of numerous race riots throughout the 1960s. Housing was in dismal shape, and it would only get worse though the 1970s. On the other hand, Harlem was a mecca for black-owned businesses; soul food stalwart Copeland's had been open nearly a decade, and Sylvia's followed close behind. Though New York's black population was no longer as concentrated in Harlem as it had been pre-WW II, it was still the center of the city's black culture.

Hamilton recalls working for numerous black-owned restaurants around Harlem before moving to M&G Diner. "It was an experience like nothing else," she said, catering to Harlem's entire population. During the day, the older folks would gather and talk over ribs and braised oxtail. Sundays were for the church crowd. But at night, they were the scene of the after parties from Harlem's clubs. "Sometimes we had to lock the door because we couldn't let any more people in," said Hamilton. At the time M&G was open 24 hours a day, so people would come in looking for breakfast food after dancing all night—salmon croquettes with cheese grits, home fries and fluffy pancakes. They could barely keep food on the griddle.

"Betty made food that was like what I made at home, but she added some things I could never figure out," said Arsolar Clemons,[214] another former M&G employee. Meats came from Smitty's Inner City Meat, a black-owned butcher on 12th Avenue that supplied many of the neighborhood's soul food eateries,[215] and Gadsden, known as "Mr. G" would do much of the shopping himself. "He was always in there," said Hamilton. "He wasn't the type to let other people take care of his business." The food, and the jukebox, attracted everyone, from club-goers to civil rights leaders like Jesse Jackson to celebrities like Stevie Wonder and Denzel Washington. The cover of Puff Daddy's single "Can't Nobody Hold Me Down" even features M&G's iconic sign.[216] And according to Hamilton, everyone was worried if they passed by and the sign's lights were off, poking their heads in and insisting they be turned on.

Fred Gadsden continued to run M&G Diner through the 1980s and 1990s, and in 1993 was one of the founding members of the 125th Street Business Improvement District. "People in Harlem still talk about his establishment that was a gathering place for good food and political conversations," wrote the BID in a newsletter.[217] By that time, Harlem had changed significantly from the 1960s. Clemons talks about catering to European tourists who read of M&G in guidebooks, looking for an authentic "black food experience," and ordering chitterlings and black-eyed peas. They were happy to serve whoever came in their doors, but as black food increasingly became a commodity (and tourist attraction), the environment that allowed it to thrive was eroding.

In 1996 the city passed the Third Party Transfer Program, which allowed the transfer of city-owned property to developers. Many of Harlem's formerly vacant, city-owned properties were soon in developers' hands, who brought in chain restaurants and businesses. Clemons recalls a lot of their late-night regulars began heading to IHOP for their pancake fix. M&G was also hit with numerous shutdowns from the Department of Health, which, while good intentioned, punished them for cooking techniques they had been using for years, like brining their famous fried chicken at the wrong temperatures.

M&G closed in 2008. "Mr. G worked up until he died," said Hamilton, and though his family continued on, the business was suffering on multiple fronts. Its iconic signage stayed on the corner for a while after it closed, but eventually made its way to Streetbird, a newer Harlem restaurant that wanted to pay homage to the food history of the neighborhood, attempting to recapture the environment that let black-owned soul food restaurants like M&G Diner thrive. Because the Harlem that made that happen is already gone.

M&G's Black-Eyed Peas

According to Pearl Hamilton, M&G made their black-eyed peas with salt pork, beans and just a little sugar. Some recipes might get more complicated than that, but really, it seems like all you need for this comforting, soul food dish.

SERVES 4 AS SIDE DISH

¼ lb (108 g) bacon or salt pork, cubed

½ lb (226 g) black-eyed peas

2 tsp (10 g) brown sugar

Salt to taste

Heat a small saucepan over medium-low heat and add the cubed pork. Cook the pork down until fat is well rendered, about 5 minutes. Add the beans to pork and mix well, then cover with water by 2 inches (5 cm). Bring to a boil, then lower heat and simmer for an hour, stirring occasionally and adding liquid if the beans start to dry out. Once beans are tender, remove from heat and stir in sugar and salt, and serve warm.

[218] For reference information see Endnotes.

M&G's Stewed Cabbage

Pearl Hamilton remembers the stewed cabbage at M&G, stewed with fried salt pork and "a little sugar." This method ensures the cabbage retains a little texture and doesn't entirely become mush, while infusing every bite with the taste of pork. It makes the perfect accompaniment to a fried chicken picnic lunch.

Serves 4 as side dish

¼ lb (113 g) salt pork or bacon, diced

2–3 cups (473–709 ml) water

1 head of cabbage, thinly sliced

1 tbsp (15 g) sugar

Salt and pepper to taste

In a large saucepan, fry the pork until it's lightly browned and the fat has started to render. Add 2 cups (473 ml) of water and bring to a boil, then add the sliced cabbage. Cover and simmer until it's tender, about another 20 minutes. Add more water if the cabbage starts to dry out. Once the cabbage is tender, uncover and bring to a boil for another minute. Remove from heat and stir in sugar, salt and pepper.

[219] For reference information see Endnotes.

M&G-Style Fried Chicken

M&G soaked their chicken in a heavily seasoned salt brine, so that "all it needed was to go in the flour and the pepper," said Pearl Hamilton. No thick batters needed here. The seasoned salt was from Smitty's, a neighborhood butcher and sadly cannot be reproduced exactly, but making brine with your favorite seasoned salt will do the trick. The result is a punch of flavor under perfectly crispy chicken skin.

SERVES 4

1 cup (240 g) seasoned salt

2 cups (473 ml) water

1 (3–5 lb [1.3–2.2 kg]) chicken

2 cups (256 g) all-purpose flour

Freshly ground black pepper to taste

Oil for frying

In a small saucepan, combine seasoned salt and water. Bring to a simmer until the salt is fully dissolved, then let cool. Butcher the chicken, leaving the skin on and submerge the chicken pieces in the brine. Cover and let marinate for 15 to 30 minutes (30 minutes if you prefer your chicken very salty). Remove the chicken from the brine, rinse and pat dry. In a large bowl or large paper bag, combine the flour and pepper. Add the chicken pieces a few at a time and shake to coat with flour and pepper, then knock off the excess and set aside.

In a deep fryer or large Dutch oven, heat enough oil to submerge the chicken to 375°F (190°C). Fry the chicken pieces a few at a time until golden brown, about 10 minutes, until they read 165°F (74°C) inside. Remove and drain on paper towels, and keep in a warm oven until ready to serve.

THE TACK ROOM

Tucson, AZ

1969-2003

———··———

Most people wouldn't expect a fine-dining establishment to advertise itself with a gigantic, concrete cowboy boot. But that's not how you do business in Arizona. The boot was originally the logo for the Rancho Del Rio "dude ranch," which was developed in 1946, a place for tourists to escape their cold winter climates and ride a few horses. In the early 1950s, owner Jud Kane realized they needed to start serving something more interesting than cold sandwich lunches to their guests, and called his sister, Alma Vactor, to head up the kitchen.

Tucson doesn't seem like the type of city where someone would have a hard time staying in business. It's not a city for hustlers like New York or San Francisco; there isn't always someone waiting in the wings to do what you did better and cheaper. And yet, in the 1960s, the bankruptcy rate was higher in Tucson than it was in New York. The problem? Seasonality. Air conditioning was still a rare treat in those days, and because of the Southwest's blistering summers, Rancho Del Rio (and most other hospitality businesses) would close from Easter through Thanksgiving.

However, the Vactors were beginning to gain a reputation for the quality of the food served at the restaurant in Rancho Del Rio, and eventually took the risk of opening a standalone restaurant, The Tack Room, in 1969, the first fine-dining establishment in Arizona. "We were in a unique part of the country. It wasn't a big city, it wasn't as cosmopolitan," explained Drew Vactor,[220] who ran the restaurant from 1974 through 2000. "We had to establish some different rules." For instance, while most high-end restaurants required a jacket and tie for men, "no one wants to wear a tie when it's 110 degrees out." The Tack Room had to balance the standards of fine dining with the expectations of the local clientele.

That was perhaps no more evident than on its menu. While it served the chateaubriand steak and roast duckling expected of any haute cuisine restaurant at the time, Drew Vactor figured they could stand out by utilizing local ingredients—something to which chefs in even the biggest dining destinations had just started catching on. "You wouldn't think in the Arizona desert you'd find anything growing but cactus," he said, "but we have great vineyards, huge pecan groves and we grow fresh melons." The menu began to reflect those flavors, with a pepper steak made with local peppers, or a rack of Colorado lamb with cilantro and mesquite honey. "When the tourists would stay here, they'd say it's the greatest meal partly because it wasn't New York or Chicago prices," said Vactor, "but for the local people it was pricey, and more of a special-occasion spot. We had to make sure we didn't chase the locals away." One way to make sure of that was the 16-food concrete cowboy boot Vactor had commissioned as a sign. If that didn't make it clear The Tack Room was about the Southwest, nothing would.

The Mobil Travel Guide (now the Forbes Travel Guide) awarded The Tack Room four stars in 1973, and then five by 1977.[221] By that point, competition had cropped up as well, mainly in hotels. According to Vactor, the hotel restaurants had an easier time than The Tack Room, given that things like valet parking, utility cost and kitchen equipment were all taken care of by the hotel. "Today if you look at the Forbes list, most of the best restaurants are in hotels, because they're the only ones who can really afford to do that," he said. "It's much more complicated if you have a single location and you have to worry about all of that yourself."

In the end it wasn't gentrification or changing tastes that did The Tack Room in, but the simple reality that running a restaurant is a hard job. Vactor was working long hours, and after bouts of illness, decided it was too much for him. He sold the restaurant in 2000, but the next owner didn't find as much success, and it closed in 2003. Today the famed concrete boot sits outside the Vactor Ranch, a gated community in Tucson. Perhaps The Tack Room would have found its end anyway, though. They may have been the first fine dining in Arizona, but as happened elsewhere, others found their way to the Southwest, ready to use local flavors, ready to do what they were doing.

TACK ROOM'S FROZEN WATERMELON SOUP

In the spirit of using local ingredients, and to satisfy diners on hot desert days, the Tack Room served this frozen watermelon soup (though actually more like a granita than anything) made from local melons. It's the rare dish that works as an appetizer or a dessert. Eat it on the hottest of days.

SERVES 4

3 cups (720 g) watermelon, seeds removed and cubed

2 tbsp (30 g) superfine sugar

1 cup (236 ml) cold sparkling mineral water

Purée melon and sugar in a food processor until smooth. Strain through a sieve into a shallow dish, and then freeze the resulting liquid until it's very firm, about an hour. Once frozen, scrape out the icy mixture into four shallow bowls, arranging the shavings into a mound. Pour an even amount of sparkling water over each mound, and serve immediately.

[223] For reference information see Endnotes.

TACK ROOM'S RICE RELISH

According to Drew Vactor, the Rice Relish was the Tack Room's version of an amuse bouche, putting a twist on haute cuisine by using local peppers. The dish is built on the combination of heat from the peppers and chilled, creamy rice. Apparently it was so popular that guests would loudly complain if they experimented with anything else.

SERVES 8

1 roasted red Anaheim pepper, peeled, seeded and chopped

1 roasted red bell pepper, peeled, seeded and chopped

½ small onion, diced

2 tbsp (30 g) carrots, diced

2 tbsp (30 g) celery, diced

¼ cup (60 g) green bell pepper, diced

⅛ tsp ham base

2 tsp (30 ml) water

¾ cup (177 ml) mayonnaise

6 tbsp (88 ml) white vinegar

2 tbsp (30 g) sugar

¼ oz (7 g) dry mustard

⅛ oz (3.5 g) salt

1–2 drops Tabasco

3 cups (720 g) cooked, chilled white rice

To roast the peppers, place them directly over a high flame on the stovetop, turning with tongs until the skin is blackened and blistering. Remove and let cool, then scrape the skin off with the back of a knife, seed and chop. Set aside.

Put the onion, carrots, celery and half of the green bell peppers into a food processor and grind together until almost smooth. In a small bowl, mix the ham base and water thoroughly and set aside. In a large bowl, combine the mayonnaise, white vinegar, sugar, dry mustard, salt, ham mixture and ground vegetables thoroughly. Stir in the roasted Anaheim pepper, red bell pepper, remaining diced green bell pepper and Tabasco.

Mix the relish into chilled white rice until completely coated. Serve as amuse bouche or side dish.

[222] For reference information see Endnotes.

TACK ROOM'S VEAL WITH CHANTERELLE MUSHROOMS

Continental dishes like this one were common on The Tack Room's menu, but a rare treat in the Southwest. This particular one was named by the Chicago Tribune *as one of the restaurant's not-to-miss dishes. Wild chanterelles do grow in Arizona, and give the veal an earthy, nutty taste, even more enhanced by the brown butter sauce.*

SERVES 4

8 slices veal (scaloppini), about 1 lb (453 g)

Salt and freshly ground pepper to taste

2 tbsp (16 g) flour

5 tbsp (75 g) butter

6 oz (170 g) fresh chanterelle mushrooms, or 2 oz (57 g) dried chanterelles (soaked in water to reconstitute)

½ cup (118 ml) dry sherry

2 tbsp (30 g) finely chopped parsley

Pound the veal slices with a flat mallet. Sprinkle them with salt and pepper and dredge lightly in flour. Shake off the excess. Heat 3 tablespoons (45 g) of butter in a heavy skillet over medium heat and add the veal. Cook for 2 to 3 minutes per side, until seared and still tender. Remove the veal to a warm platter.

Add the remaining butter to the skillet and cook, stirring. The butter will foam and then begin to smell nutty and toasty, at which point it should be the color of hazelnuts. Do not burn. If using dried chanterelles, drain from water. Add the mushrooms and the sherry to the browned butter and ignite the sauce, shaking the pan until the flames die out. Pour the mushrooms and sauce over the veal. Sprinkle with parsley, and serve.

[224] For reference information see Endnotes.

MISTER C'S

Omaha, NE

1971-2007

———·———

Mister C's was a place that knew the value of a gimmick. After all, you sort of had to have a hook if you were serving pizza in steak country, so every year Sebastiano "Yano" Caniglia, founder of Omaha mainstay Mister C's, made a habit of purchasing the AkSarBen Grand Champion Steer.[225] Though maybe this only sounds like a gimmick because it's rare to associate Italian-American cuisine with heartland beef. For the Italians in Omaha, this wasn't an issue.

Cirino and Giovanna Caniglia were originally from Sicily, and opened a bakery in Omaha's Little Italy neighborhood in 1920. They were stalwarts of the city's Italian community, which was thriving by the 1950s. Many Italians had come to work for the Union Pacific Railroad, or to work in the livestock industry, but over the years opened their own businesses. In 1941,[226] the WPA Writers' Program published *The Italians of Omaha* and described Omaha's bustling Little Italy:

"The streets of Little Italy resound with the noise and laughter of many children. The stores display foods found dear to the heart of the people—salamis, cheeses, olive oil, macaroni, spaghetti, braided lengths of garlic and strings of gleaming red peppers drying in the sun. In season, the Italians make pasta pomodoro, a highly seasoned tomato sauce, and the appetite-teasing odor of it pervades the entire neighborhood."

"The Caniglias introduced pizza to the Midwest," says David Caniglia, Yano's son.[227] "No one had heard of it before." Actually, not even the Italians knew about it—a few of the Caniglia brothers discovered it on the East Coast after returning from WW II, though their mother had been making something similar for them called "cucerne" at home. Other men were returning from the war as well, with palates for the new foods they discovered in Europe, so the Caniglias decided to turn the family bakery into Caniglia's Pizzeria in 1946.

However, in 1953 Yano opened his own restaurant, Caniglia's Royal Boy Drive-In, in North Omaha, across the street from a Naval Reserve training center. It became popular with the teens and sailors, serving "pizza burgers" and the like. Yano Caniglia expanded Royal Boy, adding an indoor dining area, and in 1971 closed the drive-in part and renamed the restaurant Mister C's. Mister C's was an Italian Steakhouse, as known for its fried ravioli as it was for its T-bone. It was also, as David Caniglia described, "a very festive dining experience. Hundreds of thousands of Christmas lights and an eclectic Italian theme set Mister C's apart from the rest." Yano and his wife Mary were also attentive hosts, coming from a family of experienced restaurateurs—every Caniglia sibling owned or was involved in at least one restaurant in Omaha for a time.

"The Italian steakhouse combination is more common than you would think," said David Caniglia. Like many immigrant populations, early Italian immigrants in the Midwest balanced assimilation with tradition, holding on to some of their customs while embracing those of their new home country. And in that balance, they often discovered something entirely new, cuisines that would be unrecognizable to their Sicilian ancestors but just as authentic. Honest cuisine comes when people take what's available to them, whether that's Parmesan cheese or prized steer, and create food they'd want to eat. It doesn't matter how "traditional" it looked, they were creating new traditions.

"After 53 years of taking care of our wonderful customers, we're going to retire by the fall of next year,"[231] said Mary Caniglia in 2006. The restaurant closed in 2007, though their sauce and dressing can still be bought at some retailers in the Midwest. There is still a thriving Little Italy in Omaha, and there are a few restaurants in Omaha with Caniglia family connections, but no more that bear the Caniglia name. "Yano Caniglia represented the American dream," said David Caniglia, that the son of immigrants with a high school education could build a beloved and successful business, and retire in peace. Not all restaurants go out with a bang.

MISTER C'S-STYLE FRIED RAVIOLI

According to David Caniglia, their fried ravioli was "breaded with Italian seasonings and served with our spaghetti sauce as dip." You can still buy Mister C's sauce at some stores around Nebraska. However, your favorite marinara sauce will also do. This approximation of Mister C's recipe makes for crispy ravioli with the lightest of coatings.

SERVES 4 AS APPETIZER

Neutral oil, for frying

1 cup (237 ml) milk

2 cups (118 g) Italian seasoned bread crumbs

24 fresh cheese ravioli, cooked and cooled

¼ cup (45 g) Parmesan cheese, shredded

Marinara sauce, for dipping

Pour 2 inches (2.5 cm) of oil in a deep frying pan. Heat over medium high heat until hot and crackling.

Put milk and bread crumbs in separate bowls. Working in batches, dip the ravioli in milk, dredge in bread crumbs, then place on a plate or baking sheet. When ready, fry the ravioli in batches until they are golden brown, about 3 minutes, turning often. Remove ravioli from oil with a slotted spoon and place on paper towels to drain. Sprinkle ravioli with cheese, and serve with marinara dipping sauce.

CORN DANCE CAFÉ

Santa Fe, NM/Shawnee, OK

1993-2003

⸻

"Native American foods have not been represented as such," said Loretta Barrett Oden,[228] founder of the Corn Dance Café. In the best cases they have been absorbed and in the worst appropriated, but overall there is a long separation between the foods native to the Americas and appreciation for what Native Americans did with them. Italy gets tomatoes, and Thanksgiving is what pumpkins and cranberries are for, and Native Americans are left with fry bread as their most visible culinary contribution. Oden wanted to breathe life and history into the public understanding of Native cuisines, and for a brief period the Corn Dance Café brought them all under one roof.

Oden is a member of the Citizen Potawatomi Nation, and born on the reservation in Shawnee, Oklahoma, where there are 39 federally recognized tribes. "We were moved here from all parts of North America, so there's influence from all over, from all of these different tribes." However, those foodways were hard to capture, especially with many Native families living off a governmental food program. "The whole commodities program, as it was even when I was growing up—I don't think anything in that box was nutritious. It was powdered milk, powdered eggs, a lot of army surplus stuff, Spam, lard. I think the dried pinto beans were the only healthy thing in the batch." In fact, the now ubiquitous fry bread was developed as a filling and palatable, but ultimately unhealthy, way to use those ingredients.

So she and her son, the late Clayton Oden, opened the Corn Dance Café in a small adobe house in Santa Fe. Their menu focused on Native-sourced, Native-produced ingredients, whether it was local bison, Minnesota wild rice or Alaska salmon, to showcase the full range of native cuisines. There were also numerous dishes showcasing the "three sisters" of American cuisine—corn, squash and beans, which were often cultivated together. "When you look at cuisine in this country, absolutely every ethnicity is represented. But Native American foods, or original foods, have really been skipped over. That's the void that we were trying to fill." It was a nearly instant hit, frequented by local natives and tourists alike, and eventually landed her a few TV spots. A development across the street for a time forced them to relocate to Santa Fe's only Native-owned hotel, where they operated for another six years, before Oden returned to Oklahoma. She briefly reopened the Corn Dance Café in Shawnee, but after a few months put more of her focus on "reintroducing my own people to food for health reasons and cultural reasons."

"I just hate politics," said Oden. "I thought, golly, there's a lot of political issues surrounding who we are as Native people, and the ugly history and all that, but I don't like that. I didn't want to go there. I wanted this to be upbeat and beautiful and sexy, and use this wonderful food as a way of informing people, very gently, of who we are." In a way, Oden may have failed, because a mission like that is inherently political. Food is the quickest way to experience the essence of another culture, and the Corn Dance Café introduced that food to a new audience—and sometimes reminded customers that foods they were already familiar with, like chocolate and okra, existed far before 1492. By making its origins explicit, the Corn Dance Café gave those origins value. If anyone enjoyed the food, they had to give recognition and credit to the people it came from. And in a country that has spent so long discrediting its Native population, that can be a revolutionary act.

CORN DANCE CAFÉ'S MOCTEZUMA'S REVENGE

Don't let the name put you off, because this spicy chocolate bread pudding is an entirely pleasant experience.
The combination of hot peppers and chocolate from South America and dried cranberries from
the North makes for a real all-American dessert.

SERVES 6

———•———

3 whole dried pasilla chiles

6 oz (170 g) dark 70% bittersweet chocolate, in pieces

3 cups (709 ml) milk

5 eggs

1 cup (200 g) brown sugar, firmly packed

½ tsp cinnamon

1 tsp (5 g) allspice

2 tbsp (30 ml) pure vanilla extract or 1 whole vanilla beans, opened and seeds scraped out

¼ cup (60 g) sun-dried cranberries, minced

¼ cup (60 g) sun-dried tart cherries, minced

6 oz (170 g) French bread or chocolate brioche, cubed

3 tbsp (45 g) unsalted butter, cut into small pieces

1 cup (240 g) pecans, finely chopped

Preheat the oven to 350°F (176°C).

Slice open the chiles and discard the seeds and stems. On a skillet over medium-high heat, toast the chiles, pressing down with a spatula until they sizzle. Transfer them to a bowl of warm water and soak until they're soft, about half an hour. Drain and discard any leftover seeds, stems or veins. Purée the chiles then strain into a small bowl.

Place the chocolate and milk into a saucepan and heat, stirring constantly, until melted. Remove from heat and set aside. In a large mixing bowl, whisk together the eggs, sugar, cinnamon, allspice, vanilla and chili purée. Slowly add in the chocolate mixture and combine. Add the cranberries, cherries and bread cubes. Take a large plate and weigh down the mixture, so that the bread is fully submerged, and let stand for half an hour.

Lightly butter a 10-inch (25.4-cm) round cake pan, at least 2–3 inch (5–7.6 cm) high. Pour pudding mixture into the pan, and top with butter pieces and chopped nuts. Bake for about 40 minutes, until a tester comes out clean. Allow to cool slightly, and serve.

CORN DANCE CAFÉ'S THREE SISTERS SAUTÉ

The "three sisters" of Native cuisine are corn, beans and squash, and they form the base of many Native recipes. This sauté uses all three, plus tomatoes and sage pesto. This fresh dish benefits from being made in the summer, when corn is at its ripest and sweetest.

SERVES 6

SAGE PESTO

1 cup (240 g) pine nuts, toasted

½ cup (118 ml) olive oil

10 cloves garlic, chopped

3 bunches sage, roughly chopped

1 bunch parsley, roughly chopped

1 tsp (5 g) salt

Juice of one lemon

1 tbsp (15 g) fresh, mild goat cheese (optional)

2 ears fresh corn

3 tbsp (45 ml) olive oil

1 lb (453 g) mixed baby squashes (patty pan, sunburst zucchini, etc.) or
1 lb (453 g) yellow and Zucchini squash, cubed

1 cup (240 g) heirloom beans, cooked

1 cup (240 g) ripe Roma tomatoes, chopped

Salt and pepper to taste

To make the pesto, toast the pine nuts in a dry sauté pan for a few minutes. Combine all the ingredients in a food processor or blender and pulse until combined and almost smooth. The pesto may be stored in a refrigerator for up to 2 weeks.

Pull the husks back but not off the corn, and remove the silks. Roast the corn over a stove gas flame until golden. Let cool and slice the kernels from the cob with a sharp knife. Heat the oil in a large sauté pan, and add the squash, cooking for about a minute. Then in succession, tossing and stirring with each addition, add the beans, corn, tomatoes, salt and pepper, and sage pesto. Stir gently to distribute evenly. Check for seasonings and serve immediately.

THREE SISTERS & FRIENDS SALAD

Quinoa, jicama, wild rice—these ingredients are all native to the "New World," and showcased beautifully in this colorful summer salad, along with the traditional "three sisters." It's a dish that exhibits just how varied New World ingredients can be, especially when they are served raw and at their freshest.

SERVES 6

1 cup (240 g) dry black beans

4 cloves garlic, minced

1 cup (240 g) uncooked quinoa

½ cup (120 g) wild rice

½ cup (120 g) green zucchini, raw, unpeeled, 1-inch (2.5-cm) dice

¼ tsp cumin seeds

½ cup (120 g) yellow zucchini or crookneck, raw, unpeeled, 1-inch (2.5-cm) dice

¼ cup (60 g) red bell peppers, seeded, deveined and ¼-inch (0.6-cm) dice

¼ cup (60 g) green bell peppers, seeded, deveined and ¼-inch (0.6-cm) dice

¼ cup (60 g) yellow or purple bell peppers, seeded, deveined and ¼-inch (0.6-cm) dice

½ cup (120 g) jicama, peeled, raw, 1-inch (2.5-cm) dice

1 whole fresh jalapeño or serrano chili, seeded, deveined and minced

½ cup (120 g) fresh cilantro leaves, stemmed & chopped

2 whole green onions, thinly sliced, with tops

⅓ cup (80 g) fresh mint leaves, minced

½ tsp kosher salt

Whole endive leaves

Mint, cilantro sprigs and chopped avocado for garnish

DRESSING

½ cup (118 ml) extra virgin olive oil

¼ cup (60 ml) seasoned rice wine vinegar

Juice from 1 lime

Rinse the black beans, then cover them with water and bring to a boil. Reduce heat and simmer them with half the minced garlic until al dente, about half an hour. Drain and set aside. (Alternately, used canned and rinsed black beans.)

Rinse the quinoa over a fine chinois or a strainer lined with cheesecloth, then cover with cold water in a small saucepan. Bring to a boil, then reduce heat and simmer, until quinoa becomes translucent and the small white endosperm appears, about 15 minutes. Drain immediately and rinse with cold water to stop the cooking. Set aside.

Rinse and cook the wild rice in boiling water until it just "blooms" but is still al dente, about 30 to 40 minutes, then drain and set aside. In a skillet, dry toast the cumin seeds until just aromatic, then remove and grind with a mortar and pestle or in a spice mill.

Whisk together all the ingredients for the dressing, then toss with the black beans and let sit for half an hour. Fluff the quinoa and wild rice together in a large mixing bowl, and toss with zucchini, peppers, jicama, jalapeño, onions, mint, kosher salt, cilantro and the dressed black beans. Adjust seasoning and add more dressing if necessary. Spoon into individual endive leaves, and top with chopped avocado, mint and cilantro.

[229] For reference information see Endnotes.

Endnotes

1   Courtesy Century Inn.

2   Courtesy Century Inn.

3   "Phantom at the Planters, 1833–1933, our first hundred years." Collection of material relating to Planters Restaurant, New-York Historical Society / Main Collection F128 TX945.5.P53 C66 1933 / Non-circulating

4   Wilkerson, Lyn. Historical Cities-New York City. N.p.: Caddo Publications, 2010. Web. 15 Nov. 2014. <https://books.google.com/books?id=MvR9Xzq2FIUC&source=gbs_navlinks_s>.

5   Parker, H. Jerome. "This Week In...New York." Woodland Daily Democrat 24 Feb. 1931: 6. Newspapers.com. Web. 10 Aug. 2015. <http://www.newspapers.com/image/52302786/>.

6   "D. Clinton Mackey, Once of Brooklyn, Dies in Plainfield." The Brooklyn Daily Eagle 19 June 1932: 12A. Newspapers.com. Web. 10 Aug. 2015. <http://www.newspapers.com/image/58211320/>.

7   New York City Guide. N.p.: Guilds' Committee For Federal Writers' Publications, n.d. American Guide Ser. WPA. Web. 10 Apr. 2015. <https://books.google.com/books?id=KEwe-UMAYWEC&printsec=frontcover#v=onepage&q&f=false>.

8   "Phantom at the Planters, 1833-1933, our first hundred years." Collection of material relating to Planters Restaurant, New-York Historical Society / Main Collection F128 TX945.5.P53 C66 1933 / Non-circulating

9   "Harvey's, Home of Steamed Oyster, Goes In Limbo." The Free Lance-Star [Fredericksburg, VA] 19 Sept. 1931, The Woman's Page sec.: n. pag. Web. 10 Nov. 2014. <https://news.google.com/newspapers?nid=1298&dat=19310919&id=HtdNAAAAIBAJ&sjid=wIoDAAAAIBAJ&pg=4922,2370569&hl=en>.

10 Chapple, Bennett. "Let's Talk It Over." National Magazine 1909: n. pag. Google Books. Web. 14 Nov. 2014. <https://books.google.com/books?id=HUQPAQAAIAAJ&dq=harvey%20steamed%20oysters&pg=PA712#v=onepage&q&f=false>.

11 Evelyn, Douglas E., Paul Dickson, and S. J. Ackerman. On This Spot: Pinpointing the past in Washington, D.C. Sterling, VA: Capital, 2008. Print.

12 "HARVEY OF FAMOUS RESTAURANT DEAD; He Fed Statesmen, Diplomats, and Celebrities in Washington for Fifty Years. CIVIL WAR MADE HIS FAME His Celebrated "Steamed Oysters" Owed Origin, It Is Said, to Expedient for Serving Quickly Hungry Soldiers." Editorial. The New York Times 6 May 1909: n. pag. HARVEY OF FAMOUS RESTAURANT DEAD. The New York Times, 06 May 1909. Web. 06 Aug. 2015. <http://query.nytimes.com/mem/archive-free/pdf?res=980CEFD61131E733A25755C0A9639C946897D6CF>.

13 DeFerrari, John. Historic Restaurants of Washington, D.C.: Capital Eats. Charleston, SC: American Palate, 2013. Print.

14 Kimmel, Ross M. "Oyster Wars: The Historic Fight for the Bay's Riches." The Maryland Natural Resource (2008): 4-6. Maryland Department of Natural Resources, Winter 2008. Web. 20 Aug. 2015. <http://www.dnr.state.md.us/naturalresource/winter2008/oyster_wars.pdf>.

15 Romer, Frank. The History of Harvey's Famous Restaurant. Washington, D.C.: Harvey's, Ca. 1946. Print.

16 Rector, George. "Cook's Tour." The Evening Independent [St. Petersburg, FL] 10 Mar. 1939, XXXII ed.: 1. Google Newspapers. Web. 7 Aug. 2015. <https://news.google.com/newspapers?id=9N5PAAAAIBAJ&sjid=r1QDAAAAIBAJ&pg=3271%2C5218273>.

17 "INDUSTRIAL DETROIT (1860–1900)." Detroit Historical Society, n.d. Web. 6 Aug. 2015. <http://detroithistorical.org/learn/timeline-detroit/industrial-detroit-1860-1900>.

18 Zunz, Olivier. "DETROIT'S ETHNIC NEIGHBORHOODS AT THE END OF THE NINETEENTH CENTURY." Diss. U of Michigan, 1977. University of Michigan Library. Web. 6 Aug. 2015. <http://deepblue.lib.umich.edu/bitstream/handle/2027.42/50936/161.pdf?sequence=1>.

20 Detroit City Directories, Volume 1. Birmingham, MI: n.p., 1879. Google Books. Web. 20 Aug. 2015. <http://books.google.com/books?id=vVniAAAAMAAJ&dq=schweizer%27s+detroit&source=gbs_navlinks_s>.

21 Woodford, Frank B., and Arthur M. Woodford. "The Lively Arts." All Our Yesterdays: A Brief History of Detroit. Detroit: Wayne State UP, 1969. 175. Print.

22 Baluch, Vivian M. "Michigan's Greatest Treasure—Its People." Editorial. The Detroit News 4 Sept. 1999: n. pag. Detnews.com. Web. 06 Aug. 2015. <http://web.archive.org/web/20071209015812/http://info.detnews.com/redesign/history/story/historytemplate.cfm?id=109>.

23 Courtesy Michael Jackman

24 "Hot Dog, Hamburger Orders Horrify At Locke-Ober." Editorial. Nashua Telegraph 31 Dec. 1970: 3. Newspapers.com. AP. Web. 06 Aug. 2015. <http://www.newspapers.com/image/751996621/>.

25 English, Bella. "Diners Mourn Closing of Venerable Locke-Ober." BostonGlobe.com. N.p., 23 Oct. 2012. Web. 20 Aug. 2015. <http://www.bostonglobe.com/metro/2012/10/22/locke-ober-leaves-legacy/J5uliknYO4puLNr3giNXEK/story.html>.

26 "Food: Finnan Haddie: Famed Boston Restaurant Contributes Directions for the American Favorite." The New York Times 20 Dec. 1955: 36. ProQuest Historical Newspapers: The New York Times with Index. Web. 7 Aug. 2015. <http://ezproxy.nypl.org/login?url=http://search.proquest.com.i.ezproxy.nypl.org/docview/113338916?accountid=35635>.

27 "Sea Food Dishes from Famous Restaurants." The High Point Enterprise 17 Apr. 1960: 8. Newspapers.com. Web. 7 Aug. 2015. <http://www.newspapers.com/image/11882787/>.

28 Murrin, John M., and Paul E. Johnson. Liberty, Equality, and Power: A History of the American People. N.p.: Thomson Learning, 2007. Print.

29 Drake, Samuel Adams, and Walter K. Watkins. Old Boston Taverns and Tavern Clubs. N.p.: W.A. Butterfield, 1917. Project Gutenberg. Web. 6 Aug. 2015. <http://www.gutenberg.org/ebooks/42999?msg=welcome_stranger#Page_73>.

30 "In Disguise. How Alcohol Figures in Drug Store Beverages." The Brooklyn Daily Eagle, 16 Feb. 1886: 1. Web. 6 Aug. 2015. <http://bklyn.newspapers.com/image/50463113/>.

31 Howerth, I. W. "The Coffee-House As Rival of the Saloon." American Magazine of Civics 1895: 589-602. Google Books. Web. 20 Aug. 2015. <https://books.google.com/books?id=mWgpAAAAYAAJ&dq=American+Magazine+of+Civics+1895&source=gbs_navlinks_s>.

32 Van Rensselaer, Howard, ed. The Albany Medical Annals. 1st ed. Vol. XVI. Albany, NY: H.B. Kimmey, 1895. Google Books. Web. 6 Aug. 2015. <https://books.google.com/books?id=cK-4AAAAIAAJ&printsec=frontcover#v=onepage&q&f=false>.

33 Szende, Peter, and Heather Rule. "Thompson's Spa: The Most Famous Lunch Counter in the World." Boston Hospitality Review (2012): 33-38. Boston University. Web. 6 Aug. 2015. <http://www.bu.edu/bhr/files/2012/11/v1n1-Thompsons-Spa.pdf>.

34 Kinkaid, Jean. "Summer Drink." Boston Daily Globe 11 Aug. 1889: 18. ProQuest Historical Newspapers [ProQuest]. Web. 7 Aug. 2015.

35 Kinkaid, Jean. "Summer Drink." Boston Daily Globe 11 Aug. 1889: 18. ProQuest Historical Newspapers [ProQuest]. Web. 7 Aug. 2015.

36 "AMERICAN FROG LEG HUNTERS EARN ABOUT $50,000 A YEAR; Chief Consumption Is in the Hotels of the Larger Cities -- How Prices Run." Editorial. The New York Times 20 Feb. 1927: 200. The New York Times. Web. 06 Aug. 2015. <http://timesmachine.nytimes.com/timesmachine/1927/02/20/98413705.html>.

37 Smits, Lee. "Rough Weather for Peche Island." Editorial. The Ludington Daily News, 16 Apr. 1969: 9. Newspapers.com. Web. 06 Aug. 2015. <http://www.newspapers.com/image/1560522/>.

38 "Obituary 2—No Title." Editorial. The New York Times, 25 Feb. 1931: 24. Web. 06 Aug. 2015. <http://timesmachine.nytimes.com/timesmachine/1931/02/25/100993037.html>.

39 "Bookbinder's Cafe Raided For $50,000 In Best Of Liquors." Philadelphia Inquirer 1921: 1+. Print.

40 "Bookbinder Dies; Ill Short Time." Trenton Evening Times, 26 Oct. 1928: 17. Print.

41 Bookbinder's Seafood House, Inc., "Bookbinder's Seafood House, Inc., Philadelphia, September 23, 1941" (1941). Restaurant Menus. Paper 105. http://scholarsarchive.jwu.edu/restaurant_menus/105

42 Stevens, William K. "BOOKBINDER'S FETE STIRS MEMORIES." Editorial. The New York Times 27 Feb. 1985: n. pag. The New York Times. Web. 06 Aug. 2015. <http://www.nytimes.com/1985/02/28/us/about-philadelphia-bookbinder-s-fete-stirs-memories.html>.

43 "An Applebee's Will Grow at Bookbinders Seafood—Philadelphia Business Journal." Philadelphia Business Journal. N.p., 24 May 2004. Web. 06 Aug. 2015. <http://www.bizjournals.com/philadelphia/stories/2004/05/24/tidbits1.html?page=all>.

44 "The Epicure: Lobster Coleman." The Atlanta Journal and the Atlanta Constitution, 13 Aug. 1950: n. pag. ProQuest Historical Newspapers [ProQuest]. Web. 7 Aug. 2015.

45 Courtesy Ronald Bookbinder

46 Courtesy Ronald Bookbinder

47 Stuart, Lettice. "Restaurateur Has Seen It All." The Times-Picayune [New Orleans, LA] 24 July 1982, Real Estate sec.: n. pag. Print.

48 Kelso, Iris. "The Cafe That Wouldn't Die." Dixie [New Orleans, LA] 6 Feb. 1983: 6. Print.

49 Heller, Dean, Hon. "CONGRATULATING ELVIRA CENOZ." Dean Heller, U.S. Senator For Nevada, 11 Sept. 2014. Web. 06 Aug. 2015. <http://www.heller.senate.gov/public/index.cfm/2014/9/congratulating-elvira-cenoz>.

50 Echeverria, Jeronima. "Ostatu Amerikanuak: The Basque-American Boardinghouse." Home Away from Home: A History of Basque Boardinghouses. Reno: U of Nevada, 1999. N. pag. Print.

51 Haller, Caryn. "Overland Says Farewell to Elvira." The Record Courier. N.p., 29 Aug. 2014. Web. 07 Aug. 2015. <http://www.recordcourier.com/news/12804403-113/overland-elvira-gardnerville-retirement>.

52 Zubiri, Nancy. "Gardnerville." A Travel Guide to Basque America: Families, Feasts, and Festivals. 2nd ed. Reno: U of Nevada, 1998. 279-84. Print.

53   "The Jaunsaras." Interview by Gretchen Holbert. Voices from Basque America. N.p., 19 Aug. 1987. Web. 7 Aug. 2015. <http://www.basque.unr.edu/oralhistory/jaunsaras/Jaunsaras.html>.

54   "Legion Auxiliary Hears Speech." *Reno Evening Gazette* 29 Mar. 1961: 10. Print.

55   "Eusebio Cenoz (in Spanish)." Interview by Mateo Osa. Voices from Basque America. N.p., 2 Dec. 1988. Web. 7 Aug. 2015. <http://www.basque.unr.edu/oralhistory/cenoz_eusebio/eusebio_cenoz_index.htm>.

56   Haller, Caryn. "Overland Says Farewell to Elvira." *The Record Courier*. N.p., 29 Aug. 2014. Web. 07 Aug. 2015. <http://www.recordcourier.com/news/12804403-113/overland-elvira-gardnerville-retirement>.

57   Alexander, Jack. "LA SERVIETTE AU COU." Editorial. New Yorker 20 Mar. 1937: n. pag. *The New Yorker.* Web. 20 Jan. 2015. <http://www.newyorker.com/magazine/1937/03/20/la-serviette-au-cou>.

58   Storz, Anne Crawford. "Memories of Automats Past: Beef Pie and Depression Cocktails; Faithful Clientele." *The New York Times* 26 Apr. 1991: n. pag. *The New York Times.* Web. 23 Aug. 2015. <http://www.nytimes.com/1991/04/26/opinion/l-memories-of-automats-past-beef-pie-and-depression-cocktails-faithful-clientele-530791.html>.

59   Lowenstein, Carol. "Memories of Automats Past: Beef Pie and Depression Cocktails." Editorial. *The New York Times* 26 Apr. 1991: n. pag. *The New York Times.* 25 Apr. 1991. Web. 06 Aug. 2015. <http://www.nytimes.com/1991/04/26/opinion/l-memories-of-automats-past-beef-pie-and-depression-cocktails-502191.html>.

60   "Plan for Action," 1971, Robert F. Byrnes collection of Automat memorabilia, Manuscripts and Archives Division, The New York Public Library

61   Robert F. Byrnes collection of Automat memorabilia, Manuscripts and Archives Division, The New York Public Library

62   Robert F. Byrnes collection of Automat memorabilia, Manuscripts and Archives Division, The New York Public Library

63   Robert F. Byrnes collection of Automat memorabilia, Manuscripts and Archives Division, The New York Public Library

65   Courtesy John DeRobertis/Derobertis' Pasticceria

66   Spoerhase, Jim. "Good, But Not Bob's." Spokane Daily Chronicle 1 May 1979: 5. Web. 6 Aug. 2015. <https://news.google.com/newspapers?nid=1338&dat=19790501&id=iSUwAAAAIBA-J&sjid=H_kDAAAAIBAJ&pg=5767,230138&hl=en>.

67   Paddleford, Clementine. "Pull Up at Chuck Wagon at Chow Time Out West." *New York Herald Tribune* 25 Aug. 1956: 7. ProQuest Historical Newspapers: *New York Tribune / Herald Tribune.* Web. 19 Aug. 2015.

69   Bob's Chili Parlor. *Spokane Daily Chronicle,* 6 Feb. 1915: 8. Print.

71   Catalog of Copyright Entries, Musical Compositions, 1891-1946. Washington: Library of Congress Photoduplication Service, 1980. Print

72   Spoerhase, Jim. "Many Originals Are Offered." Spokane Daily Chronicle 23 May 1979: 37. Newspapers.com. Web. 7 Aug. 2015. <https://news.google.com/newspapers?id=WgNMAAAAIBAJ&sjid=IPkDAAAAIBAJ&pg=7260%2C2414633>.

73   Kahn, Ava Fran., and Adam Mendelsohn. "Joseph Moskowitz and the Sountrack of Little Rumania." Transnational Traditions: New Perspectives on American Jewish History. N.p.: Wayne State UP, 2014. N. pag. Print.

75   The Moskowitz & Lupowitz Restaurant. New York: Moskowitz & Lupowitz, 1940. New York Public Library. Web. 23 Aug. 2015.

76   Drell, Adrienne. "1927." 20th Century Chicago: 100 Years, 100 Voices. Chicago: *Chicago Sun-Times,* 2000. 67. Print.

78   Savela, Martin. "Noshing At The Deli." Chicago Tribune Magazine n.d.: 15-19. Web. 6 Aug. 2015. <http://archives.chicagotribune.com/1970/03/29/page/178/article/noshing-at-the-deli>.

79   Preston, Marilynn. "Where the Victuals Are Oh so Nosh." Chicago Tribune 22 May 1976, sec. 3: 24. Web. 6 Aug. 2015. <http://archives.chicagotribune.com/1976/05/22/page/268/article/where-the-victuals-are-oh-so-nosh>.

80   Mark, Norman. "Chicago's North Side Cannot Be the Same When This Deli Goes." Editorial. Lakeland Ledger 28 Jan. 1976: 7C. Web. 6 Aug. 2015. <https://news.google.com/newspapers?id=0kdNAAAAIBAJ&sjid=xPoDAAAAIBAJ&pg=4042,7518822>.

81   McGuire, Carolyn. "Ciralsky's Aspires to Be New York-style Deli." Chicago Tribune 28 Apr. 1989, sec. 7: 28-29. Web. 6 Aug. 2015. <http://archives.chicagotribune.com/1989/04/28/page/166/article/ciralskys-aspires-to-be-new-york-style-deli>.

82   Berkow, Ira. "Blintz King Stakes out New Turf." *Dixon Evening Telegraph,* 13 Feb. 1976: 11. Newspapers.com. Web. 7 Aug. 2015. <http://www.newspapers.com/image/79935440/>.

84   Ye Old College Inn memorabilia, 1915-ca.1960, MS 526, Woodson Research Center, Fondren Library, Rice University

85   Ye Old College Inn memorabilia, 1915-ca.1960, MS 526, Woodson Research Center, Fondren Library, Rice University

86   "Then and Now: Whetting Your Whistle." *Texas Monthly,* Feb. 1983: 115+. Print.

88   Cannon, Poppy. "Fudge Pie Revisited." The Milwaukee Sentinel 11 Aug. 1967, sec. 1: 10. Google Books. Web. 6 Aug. 2015. <https://news.google.com/newspapers?id=CqdRAAAAIBAJ&sjid=RREEAAAAIBAJ&pg=6364%2C4246779>.

89   Hubbell, Sue. "THE GREAT AMERICAN PIE EXPEDITION." Editorial. *The New Yorker* 27 Mar. 1989: n. pag. Web. 06 Aug. 2015. <http://www.newyorker.com/magazine/1989/03/27/the-great-american-pie-expedition>.

90   "Call It a Day." Harrisburg Telegraph 13 Sept. 1928: 10. Newspapers.com. Web. 06 Aug. 2015. <http://www.newspapers.com/image/40890729/>.

92   Ingersoll, Ali. "Historic Restaurant Closing." Wearecentralpa.com. N.p., 18 Dec. 2014. Web. 6 Aug. 2015. <http://www.wearecentralpa.com/story/d/story/historic-restaurant-closing/15230/WmUHh8Ax-UaMr-xMksPlDQ>.

93   Courtesy Jeanne Zang

94   Courtesy Jeanne Zang

95   Dickinson, Ellen E. "New York Exchange for Women's Work." Editorial. *The Art Amateur,* June 1879: 35. JSTOR [JSTOR]. Web. 7 Dec. 2014. <http://www.jstor.org/stable/25626812>.

96   Hernández, Daisy. "A Genteel Nostalgia, Going Out of Business." *The New York Times,* 22 Feb. 2003. Web. 06 Aug. 2015. <http://www.nytimes.com/2003/02/23/nyregion/a-genteel-nostalgia-going-out-of-business.html>.

97   Greene, Gael. "Was McSorley's Worth Liberating?" *New York* Magazine 20 Dec. 1971: 124-25. Google Books. Web. 13 Jan. 2015. <https://books.google.com/books?id=6eICAAAAMBAJ&lpg=PA125&ots=mKcxpNNMpW&dq=new%20york%20women's%20exchange%20restaurant&pg=PA124#v=onepage&q&f=false>.

98   Guide to the Records of the New York Exchange for Women's Work, 1878-2003, The New-York Historical Society Library, MS 446

99   The New York Exchange for Women's Work Records, MS 446, the New-York Historical Society

100   The New York Exchange for Women's Work Records, MS 446, the New-York Historical Society

101   The New York Exchange for Women's Work Records, MS 446, the New-York Historical Society

102   Castner, Ruth C. HISTORY OF ALTRUSA INTERNATIONAL, INC. COLUMBUS, OHIO Part I: 1918 - 1996, Part II: 1996 - 2003. Rep. Columbus, OH: Altrusa Club of Columbus, 1996. Web. 7 Aug. 2015. <http://www.altrusacolumbusoh.com/images/documents/AltrusaColumbusHistory.pdf>.

103   "Maramor Restaurant to Open Branch at High and State Streets." *Ohio Jewish Chronicle,* 13 Sept. 1929: 8. Rpt. in Ohio Jewish Chronicle. N.p.: n.p., n.d. Columbus Jewish Historical Society. Web. 7 Aug. 2015. <http://www.ohiomemory.org/cdm/ref/collection/ojc/id/4834>.

104   *Hotel Monthly* 29.334-335 (1921): 58. Google Books. Web. 7 Aug. 2015. <https://books.google.com/books?id=BnRAAQAAMAAJ&printsec=frontcover#v=onepage&q&f=false>.

105   Clark, Hayes T., ed. "Serving Food--An Industry." *Columbus Today* 7.3 (1931): 7+. Columbus Metropolitan Library. Web. 7 Aug. 2015. <http://digital-collections.columbuslibrary.org/cdm/ref/collection/memory/id/38458>.

106   The Maramor, A Story About The Maramor. Columbus, OH. Maramor, 1931–1940. Columbus Metropolitan Library. Web. 7 Aug. 2015. <http://digital-collections.columbuslibrary.org/cdm/ref/collection/memory/id/9332>.

107   Notes from the Maramor, Columbus Historical Society.

108   Hines, Duncan. "Adventures in Good Eating." *The San Bernardino County Sun,* 9 Nov. 1949: 18. Newspapers.com. Web. 7 Aug. 2015. <http://www.newspapers.com/image/49379904/>.

109   Reith, Cynthia Pavey. "MARAMOR'S FLOATING ISLAND." *The Columbus Dispatch,* 21 Sept. 1994, Home Final ed., Features-Food sec.: 21. Print.

110   Edwards, Don. "Rogers Will Be Missed: An 81-Year-Old Landmark and Its Family Say Farewell." *Lexington Herald-Leader* 18 July 2004: n. pag. Print.

112   Sauceman, Fred William. The Place Setting: Timeless Tastes of the Mountain South, from Bright Hope to Frog Level. Macon, GA: Mercer UP, 2006. Print.

113   Collins, Lewis, and Richard Henry Collins. "Fayette County." Collins' Historical Sketches of Kentucky: History of Kentucky. Vol. 2. Kentucky: Collins, 1882. 175-76. Print.

114   Courtesy Barbara Harper-Bach of Bluegrass Cooking Clinic, Lexington, KY

115   Clifton's. The Clifton Tray No. 160. N.p.: Clifton's, Ca. 1940. Los Angeles Public Library.

116   Chrischilles, T. H. "Chrischilles Tells of World's Most Unique Restaurants." Kossuth County Advance [Algona, IA] 11 Mar. 1948, sec. 3: 13. Web. 25 Aug. 2015. <http://www.newspapers.com/image/1333865>.

117   Thomey, Tedd. "Stepping Out." *The Independent* [Longbeach, CA] 3 Feb. 1977: 19. Newspapers.com. Web. 25 Aug. 2015. <http://www.newspapers.com/image/25924138>.

118   Mayock, Robert S. "About Wining and Dining." Editorial. *Lodi News-Sentinel* 21 Aug. 1942: 7. Web. 06 Aug. 2015. <https://news.google.com/newspapers?id=WEYzAAAAIBAJ&sjid=l-4HAAAAIBAJ&pg=6624,2292268&hl=en>.

119   Richmond, Ray. "My Mother Was the Mistress of the Owner of Clifton's Cafeteria." LA Weekly. N.p., 20 June 2013. Web. 06 Aug. 2015. <http://www.laweekly.com/arts/my-mother-was-the-mistress-of-the-owner-of-cliftons-cafeteria-4183131>.

120   Clifton's. Clifton's Family Favorites. N.p.: Clifton's, Ca. 1980. Los Angeles Public Library. Web. 7 Aug. 2015.

121   Clifton's. Clifton's Family Favorites. N.p.: Clifton's, Ca. 1980. Los Angeles Public Library. Web. 7 Aug. 2015.

122   Clifton's. Clifton's Family Favorites. N.p.: Clifton's, Ca. 1980. Los Angeles Public Library. Web. 7 Aug. 2015.

123 Mancuso, Jo. "Oregon Historical Photo: Chef Henry Thiele & Family." Weblog post. OPB. N.p., 8 Sept. 2014. Web. 1 Mar. 2015. <http://www.opb.org/artsandlife/series/historical-photo/oregon-historical-chef-henry-thiele-family/>.

124 "Map of Portland Assembly Center, Oregon, c. 2000s.." *Densho Encyclopedia*. 10 Jul 2012, 10:44 PDT. 6 Aug 2015, 08:12 <http://encyclopedia.densho.org/sources/en-denshopd-i248-00001-1/>.

125 Armstrong, J. A. "Henry Thiele's." Dining à la Oregon; a Guide to Eating Adventures in Oregon Restaurants, Featuring Famous Recipes for Specialties of the House. Porland, Or.: J & K Pub., 1959. 31. Print.

126 Beard, James. "CHEF'S CHOICE." *The Sun* (1837-1989): 1. Apr 13 1983. ProQuest. Web. 25 Aug. 2015 .

127 "Substitute for Spud Meets with Favor at Rotary Club Lunch." *The Oregon Daily Journal* [Portland, OR] 28 Feb. 1917: 4. Newspapers.com. Web. 7 Aug. 2015. <http://www.newspapers.com/image/78331284/>.

130 Courtesy Don Coble

131 Courtesy Don Coble

132 Dwan, Lois. "The Man Who Set The Standards." *Los Angeles Times*, 10 Jan. 1982: L83. ProQuest Historical Newspapers [ProQuest]. Web. 25 Aug. 2015.

133 Perino's. Digital image. Los Angeles Public Library, n.d. Web. 16 Feb. 2015. <http://dbase1.lapl.org/dbtw-wpd/exec/dbtwpub.dll>.

134 Morgan, Neil. "Perino Serves Nothing Frozen or Ready." *Redlands Daily Facts* 13 Mar. 1970: n. pag. Newspapers.com. Web. 06 Aug. 2015. <http://www.newspapers.com/image/2209737>.

136 Johnston, Myrna. "What the Men Are Having for Lunch!" *Better Homes & Gardens*, Mar. 1963: 72+. Print.

137 "This Unique Lunch Salad Is Something to Remember." *San Antonio Express*, 30 May 1968: 33. Newspapers.com. Web. 7 Aug. 2015. <http://www.newspapers.com/image/65978527>.

138 Charlie's Café Exceptionale Collection, 1933-1982, James K. Hosmer Special Collections Library

139 Nelson, Rick. "From the Archives: A Blemished Past at Charlie's." *Star Tribune*. N.p., 27 Feb. 2015. Web. 25 Aug. 2015. <http://www.startribune.com/from-the-archives-a-blemished-past-at-charlie-s/294437551/>.

140 Charlie's Café Exceptionale Collection, Hennepin County Library Special Collections

142 Johnston, Myrna. "What the Men Are Having for Lunch!" *Better Homes & Gardens*, Mar. 1963: 72+. Print.

141 Charlie's Café Exceptionale Collection, Hennepin County Library Special Collections

143 Saunders, Louise, comp. Holiday Recipes. Minneapolis, MN: Charlie's Cafe Exceptionale, n.d. Print. Hennepin County Library Special Collections

144 "Chasen's Fadeout." Editorial. *The New Yorker* 20 Feb. 1995: 88. *The New Yorker*. Web. 25 Aug. 2015. <http://www.newyorker.com/magazine/1995/02/20/chasens-fadeout>.

145 Meares, Hadley. "The Time That Was at Chasen's." KCET. N.p., 23 July 2012. Web. 25 Aug. 2015. <http://www.kcet.org/living/food/the-nosh/in-1936-dave-chasen-was.html>.

146 Yonay, Ehud. "Chasen's: Dining With The Stars." Editorial. *Independent Press-Telegram* [Longbeach, CA] 8 July 1973: 26-29. Newspapers.com. Web. 06 Aug. 2015. <http://www.newspapers.com/image/30576055/>.

147 Thomas, Bob. "Chasen's Chili Makes 'Em Feel At Home Far Away." Editorial. *The San Bernardino County Sun* 14 Jan. 1962: D3. Newspapers.com. Web. 06 Aug. 2015. <http://www.newspapers.com/image/51567022/>.

148 Claiborne, Craig. "Chasen's Chili Celebrity Favorite." *Independent Press-Telegram* [Longbeach, CA] 28 June 1973: 11. Newspapers.com. Web. 7 Aug. 2015. <http://www.newspapers.com/image/18190040/>.

149 Greene, Bob. "Melman's Deli That Never Was." *Chicago Tribune*, 9 Oct. 1988: n. pag. Chciago Tribune. Web. 25 Aug. 2015. <http://articles.chicagotribune.com/1988-10-09/features/8802060085_1_register-restaurant-delicatessen7.

150 Bernstein, Arnie, and Michael Corcoran. "North." Hollywood on Lake Michigan: 100 Years of Chicago and the Movies. Chicago, IL: Lake Claremont, 1998. N. pag. Print.

151 "Pump Room's Host Is Dead." Editorial. *The Milwaukee Journal*, 10 Feb. 1950: 12. AP. Web. 3 Mar. 2015. <https://news.google.com/newspapers?id=YeMpAAAAIBAJ&sjid=ZyMEAAAAIBAJ&pg=5785,3393277&hl=en>.

153 "Only the Name's the Same in New Pump Room Restaurant." Editorial. *The Montreal Gazette*, 16 Mar. 1976: 39. Reuter. Web. 10 Mar. 2015. <http://news.google.com/newspapers?id=MPUhAAAAIBAJ&sjid=taEFAAAAIBAJ&pg=2201,214415>.

155 "For Fancy Eating, Try Gourmet Recipes of World-famed Chefs." *The Pantagraph* [Bloomington, IL] 2 Apr. 1951: 7. Newspapers.com. Web. 7 Aug. 2015. <http://www.newspapers.com/image/69266752/>.

156 Southern Union Gas Company. *Alamogordo Daily News*, 2 Dec. 1955: 3. Print.

154 Szathmary, Louis. "Famous Chef Offers Recipe That Kept the Elegant Happy." *The Prescott Courier*, 6 May 1980: 4B. Google Newspapers. Web. 7 Aug. 2015. <https://news.google.com/newspapers?id=jn8vAAAAIBAJ&sjid=vkwDAAAAIBAJ&pg=6807%2C1134605>.

157 Harris, Art. "Atlanta's Aunt Fanny's Cabin A Caricature of the Old South." *Sarasota Herald-Tribune* 10 Dec. 1982: 8E. Web. 6 Aug. 2015. <https://news.google.com/newspapers?id=vsEqAAAAIBAJ&sjid=PmgEAAAAIBAJ&pg=6766%2C6058679>.

158 Stafford, Bessie S. "Antiques and "farm Products" Are in Aunt Fanny's Cabin." *The Constitution* [Atlanta, GA] 27 Nov. 1941: n. pag. Tomitronics. Web. 6 Aug. 2015. <http://tomitronics.com/old_buildings/aunt%20fanny/index.html>.

159 "Aunt Fanny's Cabin Sold At Auction." *Rome News-Tribune*, 26 June 1992: 6A. Web. 6 Aug. 2015. <https://news.google.com/newspapers?id=EWUwAAAAIBAJ&sjid=ETMDAAAAIBAJ&pg=3193%2C6265931>.

160 Moore, Frank. "With A Grain of Salt." *Redlands Daily Facts*, 26 Nov. 1966: 12. Newspapers.com. Web. 25 Aug. 2015. <http://www.newspapers.com/image/694747>.

161 "Slave Theme Controversial." *The Tuscaloosa News*, 5 Dec. 1982: 20A. Web. 6 Aug. 2015. <https://news.google.com/newspapers?id=DHg0AAAAIBAJ&sjid=saUEAAAAIBAJ&pg=5542%2C1214739>.

162 Levitas, Earlyne S. Secrets from Atlanta's Best Kitchens. 4th ed. Charleston, SC: Walker, Evans & Cogswell, 1974. Print.

163 Levitas, Earlyne S. Secrets from Atlanta's Best Kitchens. 4th ed. Charleston, SC: Walker, Evans & Cogswell, 1974. Print.

164 "Sugar & Spice, Everything Nice." *The Gadsden Times*, 26 June 1958: 18. Google Newspapers. Web. 7 Aug. 2015. <https://news.google.com/newspapers?id=jLsfAAAAIBAJ&sjid=1tcEAAAAIBAJ&pg=779%2C3134598>.

170 Suchetka, Diane. "Ulysses Dearing, Restaurateur, 1st Black Man to Own Major Cleveland Restaurant: Black History Month." Cleveland.com. N.p., 16 Feb. 2012. Web. 26 Aug. 2015. <http://blog.cleveland.com/metro/2012/02/ulysses_dearing_restaurateur_w.html>.

171 "Favorite Recipes of Some Top Black Chefs." *Ebony*, Aug. 1972: 164. Google Books. Web. 7 Aug. 2015.

172 Publicity Department photographs, 1940, in the Collection on the 1939/1940 New York World's Fair. Museum of the City of New York. X2013.156.33, http://nyworldsfaircollections.tumblr.com/post/68214932129/food-at-the-fair-smorgasbord-aptly-located-in

174 Courtesy Darrell Banks

175 Courtesy Darrell Banks

176 "Brown's India House Attracts Curry Devotees For Seven Years." *Sausalito News*, 24 June 1955, Volume LXX ed.: n. pag. California Digital Newspaper Collection. Web. 6 Aug. 2015.

177 Chamberlain, Claire. "Dine amidst Bengal Tigers at India House." *The Stanford Daily*, 28 July 1978, Volume 173 A ed.: 11. The Stanford Daily Archive. Web. 6 Aug. 2015.

178 Jayasanker, Laresh. "Food And Migration In The Twentieth Century." The Routledge History of Food. Ed. Carol Helstosky. N.p.: Routledge, 2014. 313-31. Print.

179 Jayasanker, Laresh. "Sameness in Diversity: Food Culture and Globalization in the San Francisco Bay Area and America, 1965-2005." Diss. The U of Texas at Austin, 2008. Web. 6 Aug. 2015. <http://www.lib.utexas.edu/etd/d/2008/jayasankerl43080/jayasankerl43080.pdf>.

180 Dixon, Naomi, and Estelle Bogg. "Pukka Sahib Dining." *The Stanford Daily*, 17 July 1981, Volume 179 A ed.: 18. The Stanford Daily Archive. Web. 6 Aug. 2015.

181 "Meatball Curry from S.F. Recipe." *The Times* [San Mateo, CA] 24 Apr. 1963: n. pag. Newspapers.com. Web. 7 Aug. 2015. <http://www.newspapers.com/image/51966634>.

182 Department of Obstetrics and Gynecology, University of California, San Franscico, comp. A Book of Favorite Recipes. Kansas City, MO: Circulation Service, 1970. Print.

184 Silva, Catherine. "Racial Restrictive Covenants." Seattle Civil Rights & Labor History Project. University of Washington, 2009. Web. 06 Aug. 2015. <http://depts.washington.edu/civilr/covenants_report.htm>.

186 "Matriarch of Seattle Chinese Community Also a Politician." Editorial. *Sarasota Herald-Tribune*, 6 June 2008: 108. Web. 06 Aug. 2015. <https://news.google.com/newspapers?id=m_QeAAAAIBAJ&sjid=X4YEAAAAIBAJ&pg=2667,494648>.

187 "Ruby Chow Quits." *Ellensburg Daily Record*, 7 Aug. 1979: 3. Web. 6 Aug. 2015. <https://news.google.com/newspapers?id=b1hUAAAAIBAJ&sjid=4Y4DAAAAIBAJ&pg=1437%2C2513880>.

188 "Ruby Chow's Bankrupt." *Ellensburg Daily Record*, 19 Sept. 1980: 5. Web. 6 Aug. 2015. <https://news.google.com/newspapers?id=0IdUAAAAIBAJ&sjid=Qo8DAAAAIBAJ&pg=5316%2C5968182>.

189 "Ruby Chow's Chinese Dinner Club." Ford Treasury of Favorite Recipes from Famous Eating Places. Comp. Nancy Kennedy. New York: Simon and Schuster, 1955. 232. Print.

191 Starr, Ken, "Golden Dreams: California in an Age of Abundance, 1950-1963," p. 103, https://books.google.com/books?id=ZWy4TexzsScC&pg=PA103&dq=paoli%27s+restaurant&hl=en&sa=X&ei=WYjrVMOyMKOxsAS4xYGYBw&ved=0CFIQ6AEwBg#v=onepage&q=paoli&f=false

192 Gumina, Deanna Paoli, "Provincial Italian Cuisines: San Francisco Preserves Italian Heritage," The Argonaut, Vol. 1 No. 1, Spring 1990, http://foundsf.org/index.php?title=Provincial_Italian_Cuisines:_San_Francisco_Conserves_Italian_Heritage

193 Courtesy Rita Paoli/Deanna Paoli Gumina.

194 Restaurants, Paoli's ca. 1970. San Francisco Ephemera Collection, San Francisco Public Library

196 Cave, Damien. "A Deli Destination, Now a Pastrami-Scented Memory." *The New York Times*. N.p., 1 Apr. 2008. Web. 07 Aug. 2015. <http://www.nytimes.com/2008/04/01/us/01miami.html?_r=1&>.

197 Courtesy of Robin Sherwood from the Wolfie Cohen family archives.

198 "Famous Cheese Cake Recipe." *Reading Eagle*, 13 Feb. 1959: 11. Google Newspapers. Web. 7 Aug. 2015. <https://news.google.com/newspapers?id=LeciAAAAIBAJ&sjid=ypsFAAAAIBAJ&pg=5725%2C5444746>.

199   Curtis, Wayne. "Tiki's Ohio Ohana." *Imbibe,* Sept.-Oct. 2014: 28. Print.

200   Motz, Doug. "History Lesson: The History of Columbus' Most Famed 'lost' Restaurant – The Kahiki." Weblog post. Columbus Underground. N.p., 11 Sept. 2012. Web. 9 Jan. 2015. <http://www.columbusunderground.com/history-lesson-the-history-of-columbus-most-famed-lost-restaurant-the-kahiki>.

201   Humuhumu. "Kahiki Supper Club." Weblog post. Humuhumu's Critiki. N.p., 2010. Web. 6 Aug. 2015. <http://critiki.com/location/?loc_id=33>.

202   Curtis, Wayne. "The Tiki Wars." *The Atlantic.* Atlantic Media Company, 01 Feb. 2001. Web. 06 Aug. 2015. <http://www.theatlantic.com/magazine/archive/2001/02/the-tiki-wars/302084/>.

203   Motz, Doug. "History Lesson: The History of Columbus' Most Famed 'lost' Restaurant – The Kahiki." Weblog post. Columbus Underground. N.p., 11 Sept. 2012. Web. 9 Jan. 2015. <http://www.columbusunderground.com/history-lesson-the-history-of-columbus-most-famed-lost-restaurant-the-kahiki>.

204   Lee, Liana. "Kahiki's Tahitian Mermaid." *The Columbus Dispatch,* 3 Jan. 2001, Home Final ed.: 2B. Columbus Dispatch Archives. Web. 9 Aug. 2015.

205   "CHICKEN PINEAPPLE KAHIKI." *The Columbus Dispatch,* 25 Aug. 2010, Home Final ed., Food sec.: 2D. The Columbus Dispatch Archive. Web. 9 Aug. 2015.

207   Knott, Andy. "Restaurant Closes Its Doors to an Era." *Chicago Tribune,* 29 Mar. 1982, sec. 1: 3. Web. 16 Mar. 2015. <http://archives.chicagotribune.com/1982/03/29/page/3/article/restaurant-closes-its-doors-to-an-era#text>.

208   "Bertrand Goldberg." Bertrand Goldberg. N.p., n.d. Web. 26 Aug. 2015. <http://bertrandgoldberg.org/>.

209   Tusa, Rosa. "Chicago to Import La Belle Epoque." *The Milwaukee Sentinel,* 5 Dec. 1963, sec. 3: 4. Google Newspapers. Web. 7 Aug. 2015. <https://news.google.com/newspapers?id=-jQqAAAAI BAJ&sjid=0E4EAAAAIBAJ&pg=7272%2C556562>.

210   Tusa, Rosa. "Chicago to Import La Belle Epoque." *The Milwaukee Sentinel,* 5 Dec. 1963, sec. 3: 4. Google Newspapers. Web. 7 Aug. 2015. <https://news.google.com/newspapers?id=-jQqAAAAI BAJ&sjid=0E4EAAAAIBAJ&pg=7272%2C556562>.

211   Tusa, Rosa. "Chicago to Import La Belle Epoque." *The Milwaukee Sentinel,* 5 Dec. 1963, sec. 3: 4. Google Newspapers. Web. 7 Aug. 2015. <https://news.google.com/newspapers?id=-jQqAAAAI BAJ&sjid=0E4EAAAAIBAJ&pg=7272%2C556562>.

213   Williams, Timothy. "Stick a Fork in Harlem Soul Food? It Seems Done." City Room. *The New York Times,* 12 Nov. 2008. Web. 06 Aug. 2015. <http://cityroom.blogs.nytimes.com/2008/11/12/stick-a-fork-in-harlem-soul-food-it-seems-done/?_r=0>.

215   "Searching for meaty profits." The Free Library. 1993 Earl G. Graves Publishing Co., Inc. 06 Aug. 2015. http://www.thefreelibrary.com/Searching+for+meaty+profits.-a013807958

216   "A Hip-Hop Hopeful." *Newsweek.* N.p., 14 Mar. 1999. Web. 06 Aug. 2015. <http://www.newsweek.com/hip-hop-hopeful-163852>.

217   "Save the Date. 125th Street BID's 19th Annual Meeting." *125th St. BID Newsletter* (May 2012): n. pag. Web. 26 Aug. 2015. <http://archive.constantcontact.com/fs055/1104232497583/archive/1109818042576.html>.

218   Courtesy Pearl Hamilton.

219   Courtesy Pearl Hamilton

221   Gaspar, John. "Neither Cowboys Nor Gourmets Will Go Hungry." *Chicago Tribune,* 29 Mar. 1987: n. pag. *Chicago Tribune.* Web. 26 Aug. 2015. <http://articles.chicagotribune.com/1987-03-29/travel/8701240505_1_mobil-travel-guide-restaurant-gourmet/?_r=0>.

222   Courtesy Drew Vactor

223   Courtesy Drew Vactor

224   Courtesy Drew Vactor

225   "Mr. C's Purchases Ak-Sar-Ben Champ." *The Lincoln Star,* 28 Sept. 1973: 5. Newspapers.com. Web. 26 Aug. 2015. <http://www.newspapers.com/image/66676410>.

226   Truax, Sue Story. "Yano Caniglia Was the Mister in Mr. C's Steakhouse." Omaha.com. N.p., 14 Nov. 2013. Web. 06 Aug. 2015. <http://www.omaha.com/go/yano-caniglia-was-the-mister-in-mr-c-s-steakhouse/article_83fcca3c-6374-55bb-9663-1cd5d7396749.html>.

229   Courtesy Loretta Barret Oden

230   Coker Ernest. "Some Pages from the Recipe Collection of Ernest Coker." (1960) Rice University: http://hdl.handle.net/1911/26744

231   "Omaha Landmark to Close in 2007." *Omaha World-Head,* 25. Nov 2006. n. pag. Print.

332   Courtesy Lou Tortorich

PHOTO CREDITS

Century Inn (9,11,12); Collection of the New-York Historical Society (15); Library of Congress Prints and Photographs Division Washington, D.C. 20540 USA dcu (19, 22); Detroit News Collection, Walter P. Reuter Library (27); Boston Public Library (33, 39); University of Windsor Leddy Library (43); Ronald Bookbinder (45, 47, 48); Ernst Cafe (53); *Nevada* Magazine (59); Photographic Collection, Miriam and Ira D. Wallach Division of Art, Prints and Photographs, The New York Public Library, Astor, Lenox and Tilden Foundations (61); Photo by Percy Loomis Sperr (c) Milstein Division. The New York Public Library (69); Northwest Museum of Arts & Culture/Eastern Washington State Historical Society, Charles Libby Photograph Collection, L87-1.38247-29 and L87-1.30253-25 (73); Gary Craig (75, 77); Chicago Jewish Historical Society (79, 80), Digital Commonwealth (83), Jeanne Zang (91, 92, 95); Columbus Metropolitan Library (105); Kentucky Historical Society (113); Los Angeles Public Library (117, 133); Richard Engeman (123, 126); Martha Blakeney Hodges Special Collections and University Archives, University of North Carolina at Greensboro (129); The Hennepin Historical Society (139, 142, 144); Elizabeth Taylor and Eddie Fisher, *Los Angeles Times* Photographic Archive, Library Special Collections, Charles E. Young Research Library, UCLA (147); Georgia State University Library (159); Tracey McCorrey (165); Darrell Banks (167); Personal collection of the author (173, 195); *Seattle Post-Intelligencer* Collection, Museum of History & Industry, Seattle (179); Deanna Paoli Gumina (181, 185); Robin Sherwood (187, 190); Geoffrey Goldberg (201, 204, 207); Ben Shirai (209); David Caniglia (221)

Food photography by Jennifer Blume

ACKNOWLEDGMENTS

Writing a book of this magnitude required a lot of time and research, which would not have been possible without considerable help. First and foremost I'd like to thank the New-York Historical Society and First We Feast, without whose partnership this project would have never have existed. Thank you to my agent, Kate McKean, for fielding endless emails that mostly boiled down to "Help! How do I write a book?" and to my editor, Marissa Giambelluca, for your ongoing encouragement.

I would also like to thank my mother, Beth Johnson, and my dear friend Victoria Pratt for helping me test some of these recipes, and all of my family and friends for their support, inspiration and enthusiasm.

Lastly, I want to thank everyone I got to speak to and interview for this book. Thank you for sharing your and your family's stories with me, and for letting me share them.

ABOUT THE AUTHOR

Jaya Saxena is a writer whose work can be found in many places across the Internet. She is the co-author of *Dad* magazine, and co-founder of Uncommon Courtesy. She lives in New York with her husband and two ungrateful cats.

INDEX